IN OTHER WORDS

Erato, Muse of Lyric Poetry
From a painting by Charles Meynier (1763-1832)

IN OTHER WORDS

SELECTED POEMS IN TRANSLATION

BILINGUAL EDITION

With adaptations in English verse
by
John E. Tidball

BISHOPSTON EDITIONS

Copyright © 2025 by John E. Tidball
Bishopston Editions, Bristol. England
All rights reserved
ISBN 978-1-9191772-3-6

CONTENTS

INTRODUCTION   7

PIERRE DE RONSARD (1524 –1585)
Ode to Cassandra   19
Sonnet for Helen   21

JOHANN WOLFGANG VON GOETHE (1749 –1832)
Welcome and Farewell   25
The Elf King   27

ALPHONSE DE LAMARTINE (1790-1869)
Solitude   31
The Lake   35

VICTOR HUGO (1802 – 1885)
Tomorrow, when the dawn…   43
Dawn is less clear…   45
Oceano Nox   47
Atonement   51

CHARLES BAUDELAIRE (1821–1867)
The Albatross   63
Correspondences   65
Reflection   67
The Balcony   69
Invitation to a Journey   71
To a Passer-by   75
A Parisian Dream   77
The Voyage   81

CONTENTS

STÉPHANE MALLARMÉ (1842 – 1898)
The Afternoon of a Faun	95
Album Leaf	103

PAUL VERLAINE (1844 – 1896)
The Art of Poetry	107
Autumn Song	111
My Familiar Dream	113
A Sentimental Colloquy	115
It weeps in my heart…	117

ARTHUR RIMBAUD (1854 –1891)
The Sleeper in the Valley	121
The Drunken Boat	123

Alphabetical index	131

INTRODUCTION

Pierre de Ronsard (1524 –1585) was one of the most important French poets of the 16th century. His vast corpus of work includes *Les Amours de Cassandre (1552)* and *Sonnets pour Hélène (1578)*, from each of which the two poems in this anthology are taken. In his collections of lyric poetry, Ronsard first used the form of the ode, as in *Ode to Cassandra*, but he later adopted the sonnet form and the alexandrine metre, as in the *Sonnet for Helen*.

Ronsard played a central role in the French Renaissance. He was the leader of a group of poets known as *La Pléiade*, who sought to elevate the French language and its literature to the level of the classics. His poetry is characterised by its formal elegance, lyrical beauty, and passionate expression. He wrote on a wide range of themes, including love, nature, mythology, and politics. His work was deeply influenced by the classical authors of Greece and Rome, as well as by the Italian Renaissance poets such as Petrarch and Torquato Tasso.

Ronsard's influence on French poetry was profound and lasting. He helped to establish French as a major literary language and expanded the possibilities of poetic expression. While his work was largely forgotten in the centuries following his death, he was rediscovered in the 19th century and is now recognised as one of the most important French poets of all time. His sonnets and odes continue to be studied and enjoyed today for their musicality and exploration of universal human themes.

Johann Wolfgang von Goethe, (1749 –1832), was a German poet, novelist, dramatist, politician and natural scientist. He is widely considered to be the most important writer in the German language. In 1770, Goethe left his home city of Frankfurt to pursue his studies at the University of Strasbourg. It was here that he met Johann Gottfried Herder. The two became close friends, and Herder kindled his interest in the notion of *Volkspoesie* (folk poetry).

On a trip to the village of Sessenheim in October 1770, Goethe fell in love with Friederike Brion, the young daughter of the local vicar, but the relationship ended in August 1771. One of his most famous poems, *Willkommen und Abschied (Welcome and Farewell)*, dates from

INTRODUCTION

this period.

In 1782, Goethe wrote what has become his most famous poem, the ballad *Erlkönig*. A young boy is carried at night by his father on horseback. The opening line tells that the time is late and that it is windy. As the poem unfolds, the boy tells his father that he can see and hear the Erlkönig (The Elf King). His father tries to comfort his son, telling him that it's just the mist, the rustling leaves, or the old willows. The Elf King tries to lure the child into joining him, with the promise of amusing games and the attentions of his daughters. Finally, the Elf King declares that he will take the boy by force. The boy cries out that he has been attacked, spurring the father to ride faster to reach their home. When they arrive, the child is dead in his father's arms. The poem has been set to music by several composers, but Schubert's impressive setting is the most widely known.

Alphonse De Lamartine (1790-1869) was a French author, poet, and statesman who was instrumental in the foundation of the French Second Republic. As one of the first French romantic poets, he is most famous for his partly autobiographical poem, *Le Lac (The Lake)*. The poem is one of several written between 1815 and 1820, when his first collection, *Les Méditations poétiques*, was published. The other poem in this anthology, *L'Isolement (Solitude)*, also dates from this period. Both poems evoke the theme of lost love, which was a typical theme of the Romantic period.

L'isolement (Solitude) conveys the speaker's profound sense of isolation and longing. It follows a journey from the natural world to the speaker's inner turmoil. The melancholic tone and elegiac imagery are characteristic of Romantic poetry, capturing the era's propensity for introspection and its fascination with nature. The poem is a poignant exploration of the themes of loss, longing, and the search for meaning in a world perceived as empty and indifferent. It showcases Lamartine's mastery of language and his ability to capture the complexities of human emotion.

Le Lac (The Lake) reflects the Romantic theme of transience and the fleeting nature of time. It expresses the speaker's regret for the passing of a cherished moment shared on the lake with a loved one.

INTRODUCTION

The speaker's thoughts and emotions unfold in stanzas that alternate between the present and the past, creating a sense of nostalgia and longing. The language is rich and evocative, with vivid descriptions and metaphors that create a powerful sense of place and mood. The poem's rhythm and rhyme scheme contribute to its lyrical quality and enhance its emotional impact.

Both poems consist of quatrains that rhyme ABAB, each quatrain having four alexandrines, lines of twelves syllables, each consisting of two hemistiches of six syllables, except that in *Le Lac* the fourth line of each quatrain consists of a single hemistich, which serves to enhance the atmosphere of stillness and serenity that the poem evokes.

Although his best-known works outside France are the novels *Notre Dame de Paris* and *Les Misérables*, **Victor Hugo** (1802–1885) was also a prolific poet, publishing several extensive collections during his lifetime. He exerted a very strong influence on the Romantic movement and the formulation of its values in France.

The famous poem that begins with the words *Demain, dès l'aube* is generally accepted to be an elegy to Hugo's daughter Léopoldine, who drowned at the age of nineteen in a boating accident on the river Seine in 1843. The poet's preoccupation with his thoughts and the shutting out of his physical surroundings portray an intense internal struggle and a profound emotional connection with his ultimate destination. The untitled poem that begins *L'aube est moins claire* laments the end of summer and the fleeting nature of time. Hugo evokes in elegiac fashion the warm summer days, the azure skies, the flowers and the birds seen on long country walks. *Oceano Nox* laments the loss at sea of ships and their crews. The title of the poem comes from a phrase in Virgil's Aeneid: *et ruit oceano nox (and night rushes upon the ocean)*.

L'Expiation (Atonement) is a very long narrative poem in seven parts, portraying the downfall of Napoleon Bonaparte. Parts one and two are included in the present edition. Part one describes in vivid detail the retreat from Moscow in 1812. Part two graphically portrays the disaster of the battle of Waterloo. The succession of

INTRODUCTION

rhyming alexandrine couplets evokes the horror of war and the end of an empire.

The most celebrated work of **Charles Baudelaire** (1821 – 1867), *Les Fleurs du mal (The Flowers of Evil)*, was first published in 1857 as a collection of a hundred poems. Following a successful prosecution for offending against public morality, six of the poems were condemned and prohibited from future publication. A new edition, which lacked the banned poems but contained several new pieces, was published in 1861. A third, augmented edition was published posthumously in 1868 by two of Baudelaire's friends, Théodore de Banville and Charles Asselineau.

Baudelaire's work influenced a generation of poets including Paul Verlaine, Arthur Rimbaud and Stéphane Mallarmé. His relatively small output, compared to that of some of his contemporaries, bears witness to the painstaking, self-critical approach that he applied to his work. More than a hundred and fifty years after his death, the universal fascination with Baudelaire's poetry shows no sign of abating.

The present collection includes six of Baudelaire's most beloved poems, which need no commentary: *L'Albatros, Correspondances, Recueillement (Reflection), Le Balcon (The Balcony), L'Invitation au voyage* and *À une Passante (To a Passer-by)*. *Rêve parisien (A Parisian Dream)* offers us a vision of Paris as seen in a dream. It illustrates the power of the poet's imagination and his desire to escape from the grim reality of his daily existence. The dream of an idyllic palace with its lakes and waterfalls is brought to an abrupt end when the poet awakes to the reality of the sordid hovel in which he lives. The last two stanzas contrast brutally with the dreamlike atmosphere of the preceding thirteen.

Le Voyage, the final poem in the present anthology, is also the final poem of the second edition of *Les Fleurs du mal*, which was published in 1861. Written during a long stay in Honfleur in 1859, it is also the longest poem in the collection. It explores the themes of wanderlust, disillusionment, and human desire. The first section introduces the restless spirit, eager to explore the vastness of the world. But

INTRODUCTION

the poet finds that this youthful idealism is often tempered by the harsh realities of life. The poem reflects the disillusionment of the era, when the grand ideals of Romanticism were giving way to a more sceptical and pragmatic view of the world. It also captures the tension between the desire for adventure and the inevitability of disappointment, a theme that would continue to resonate in much of the literature that was to follow.

Stéphane Mallarmé (1842–1898) was a major French symbolist poet. His work provided inspiration for many other poets, artists and musicians of the late nineteenth and early twentieth centuries.

Narrated by the Faun, a mythological rural deity represented as a man with the ears, horns and tail of a goat, *L'Après-midi d'un Faune (The Afternoon of a Faun)* explores the faun's longing for two beautiful nymphs, and his realisation that his desires are merely an illusion. In richly lyrical language, the poet dwells on the theme of beauty and the elusive nature of reality, reflecting the symbolist movement's focus on subjectivity and the exploration of inner landscapes. The poem inspired the composer Claude Debussy to write his symphonic poem for orchestra *Prélude à l'après-midi d'un faune* (1894), which remains to this day a classic of the musical repertoire. The legendary dancer Vaslav Nijinsky choreographed and performed the title role in a ballet of the same name, first performed in Paris in 1912.

The charming little poem *Feuillet d'album (Album Leaf)* portrays the interplay between language, music, and beauty, and the concept that art has its limits. The speaker attempts to play his flutes for a young girl, but finds that her laughter is more expressive than his music. This leads him to question the value of his music, which cannot equal the natural beauty of the human voice. The playful, quasi archaic use of language adds to the charm of the poem.

Paul Verlaine (1844 – 1896) was a French poet of the Symbolist and the Decadent movements. He is generally regarded as one of the great figures of late nineteenth century French poetry. In his poem *Art poétique (The Art of Poetry)* Verlaine playfully instructs fellow

INTRODUCTION

poets in the art of writing poetry. He tells them that they should be careful in their choice of words and avoid false sounding rhymes. They should eschew sarcasm, embellishment, and bombast. Imagery should be vague, and colours muted, and above all poetry should possess an ethereal, musical quality, achieved by using an odd number of syllables per line. Each line of the poem has nine syllables, with four syllables followed by five, with a very effective use of the mute *e*, which always counts as a syllable in French poetry when followed by a consonant.

Chanson d'automne is one of the best known of all French poems. It has been set to music several times, notably by Charles Trénet and Serge Gainsbourg, who incorporated some of the lines into one of his compositions. Lines from the poem were even used as code for the armed forces when preparing for D-Day in June 1944. The poem has visual appeal on the written page and a beautiful musicality when read aloud. Lines one and two and lines four and five of each stanza are rhyming couplets of four syllables, while lines three and six have just three syllables and rhyme with each other. When read aloud the words simply flow as a unified whole, echoing the advice of *Art poétique*.

Mon Rêve Familiar (My Familiar Dream) explores the theme of idealised love. The poet has a recurring dream about a mysterious woman who loves and understands him, offering him solace and relief from his sorrows. The poem reflects the social and cultural climate of the late 19th century, when the pursuit of romantic love and the idealisation of women was prevalent. Its dreamlike, ethereal tone portrays the subjective nature of the dream world, a theme that was dear to the disciples of the Symbolist movement. The central motif of the unknown woman symbolises the speaker's unattainable desire for perfection, and the illusion of finding perfection in love. The description of the mysterious woman conveys a sense of familiarity that suggests she is a composite of past loves, an ideal woman who exists only in the speaker's imagination.

Colloque Sentimental (A Sentimental Colloquy) presents a haunting dialogue between the ghosts of two former lovers, who meet at night in a deserted park. Their once vibrant relationship is now a mere

INTRODUCTION

ghostly echo as they encounter each other in this desolate nocturnal setting. The stark, minimalist style, with each stanza consisting of one decasyllabic rhyming couplet, reflects the bleakness and silence of the setting. The first spectre invokes the passion of their erstwhile relationship in a series of questions, while the second spectre responds in a detached, quasi mechanical manner that reflects the passage of time and the loss of love. The park itself, once a place of joy, is now deserted and frozen, reflecting the emptiness of their broken relationship.

The untitled poem that begins with the words *Il pleure dans mon coeur* expresses deep anguish and sorrow felt by the poet. The constant rain symbolizes the unrelenting pain in the speaker's heart. Rather than a torrent of grief, the long, drawn-out vowel sounds evoke a dreary, constant rain that eats away at the soul. The melancholic mood of the poem reflects the *mal du siècle*, the disillusionment and pessimism that pervaded much of 19th century French poetry from Lamartine to Apollinaire. With its simple structure of four quatrains, of which each line resembles a hemistich, or half an alexandrine, the sadness felt by the poet is enhanced by the repetition of the long rhyming vowel sounds of lines one, three and four. In an unusual departure from standard prosody, there is nothing that rhymes with line two of each stanza.

Arthur Rimbaud (1854–1891) was a French symbolist poet known for his transgressive and surreal themes and for his influence on modern literature and the arts. After his retirement as a writer in 1875 at the age of just twenty-one, he travelled extensively as a merchant and explorer until his death from cancer just after his thirty-seventh birthday.

Le Dormeur du val (The Sleeper in the Valley) is a sonnet written by Arthur Rimbaud at the age of 16. It is one of the poet's best-known poems. Written in the classical style of rhyming alexandrines, it is still far from the modernity of *Une saison en enfer* or *Illuminations*, the poet's last works, or even the audacity of the images of *Le Bateau ivre*, composed just a year later. *Le Dormeur du val* remains nonetheless a very accomplished poem, showing a mastery of the rules of prosody

INTRODUCTION

for someone who was barely sixteen years of age at the time. It is powerfully evocative in its contrast between the softness of the idyllic setting and the chilling last line.

Le Bateau ivre (The Drunken Boat), written by Rimbaud in 1871 when he was just seventeen years old, is a long poem that describes the adventures of a drifting boat in a fragmented first-person narrative replete with vivid imagery and symbolism. The one hundred lines of the poem are woven around the delirious visions of the eponymous boat. The narrator is the boat itself, recounting various experiences that include some of the purest and most transcendent visions, and at the same time some of the most repellent.

Editorial Note:

The American poet and translator Jackson Mathews wrote in 1959: "To translate a poem whole is to compose another poem. A whole translation will be faithful to the matter, and it will approximate the form of the original; and it will have a life of its own, which is the voice of the translator". The English versions in this collection are therefore conceived as adaptations rather than exact translations, as the "borrowed muse" of the original poet, so to speak. The original rhyme schemes and meters have been preserved as far as possible, in order to preserve the overall tone of the original poems.

John E. Tidball, August 2024

To Valerie
In Loving Memory

Engraving of Ronsard by Johann Theodor de Bry, 1627

PIERRE DE RONSARD (1524 –1585)

From a painting by Benjamin Foulon

À CASSANDRE

Mignonne, allons voir si la rose
Qui ce matin avoit desclose
Sa robe de pourpre au Soleil,
A point perdu ceste vesprée
Les plis de sa robe pourprée,
Et son teint au vostre pareil.

Las ! voyez comme en peu d'espace,
Mignonne, elle a dessus la place
Las ! las ses beautez laissé cheoir !
Ô vrayment marastre Nature,
Puis qu'une telle fleur ne dure
Que du matin jusques au soir !

Donc, si vous me croyez, mignonne,
Tandis que vostre âge fleuronne
En sa plus verte nouveauté,
Cueillez, cueillez vostre jeunesse :
Comme à ceste fleur la vieillesse
Fera ternir vostre beauté.

ODE TO CASSANDRA

Come, my sweet Love, to see the rose
That but this morning did unclose
Its robe of crimson to the sun.
Can it have lost, this vesper hour,
The folds of its fair-scented flower,
Pink-blushing like my fairest one?

Alas, see here upon the ground
The crimson petals all around,
So negligently cast aside.
O Nature, whence this wanton duty
To cause a flower to shed its beauty
'Twixt dawn's first light and eventide?

My Love, heed now these words, I pray:
So long as you are blithe and gay
And your sweet youth is in full bloom,
Be sure to cherish every hour,
For careless time, as with this flower,
Will mar your beauty all too soon.

SONNET POUR HÉLÈNE

Quand vous serez bien vieille, au soir à la chandelle,
Assise aupres du feu, devidant et filant,
Direz chantant mes vers, en vous esmerveillant,
Ronsard me celebroit du temps que j'estois belle.

Lors vous n'aurez servante oyant telle nouvelle,
Desja sous le labeur à demy sommeillant,
Qui au bruit de mon nom ne s'aille resveillant,
Benissant vostre nom de louange immortelle.

Je seray sous la terre et fantôme sans os
Par les ombres myrteux je prendray mon repos :
Vous serez au fouyer une vieille accroupie.

Regrettant mon amour et vostre fier desdain.
Vivez, si m'en croyez, n'attendez à demain :
Cueillez dés aujourd'huy les roses de la vie.

SONNET FOR HELEN

When you are very old, reclining in your chair
Beside the fire, unwinding wool at close of day,
Singing my verses, you in wonderment will say,
Ronsard did honour me when I was young and fair.

There is no servant who, hearing such wonders told,
Though weary from the toilsome duties of the day,
Would not wake from her sleep and rise from where she lay
To celebrate a name that Ronsard once extolled.

And when beneath the earth my mortal soul is laid
In everlasting peace beneath the myrtle's shade,
You'll sit beside the fire, a spinster bowed and bent,

Regretting that you spurned my love so long ago.
Youth is a verdant field where fragrant flowers grow:
Gather your roses now, wait not till life is spent.

Goethe bids farewell to Friederike Brion
Woodcut c. 1890 after a drawing by Eugen Klimsch (1839–1896)

JOHANN WOLFGANG VON GOETHE (1749 –1832)

From a painting by Joseph Karl Stieler

WILLKOMMEN UND ABSCHIED

Es schlug mein Herz, geschwind, zu Pferde!
Es war getan fast eh gedacht.
Der Abend wiegte schon die Erde,
Und an den Bergen hing die Nacht;
Schon stand im Nebelkleid die Eiche
Ein aufgetürmter Riese, da,
Wo Finsternis aus dem Gesträuche
Mit hundert schwarzen Augen sah.

Der Mond von einem Wolkenhügel
Sah kläglich aus dem Duft hervor,
Die Winde schwangen leise Flügel,
Umsausten schauerlich mein Ohr;
Die Nacht schuf tausend Ungeheuer,
Doch frisch und fröhlich war mein Mut:
In meinen Adern welches Feuer!
In meinem Herzen welche Glut!

Dich sah ich, und die milde Freude
Floß von dem süßen Blick auf mich;
Ganz war mein Herz an deiner Seite
Und jeder Atemzug für dich.
Ein rosenfarbnes Frühlingswetter
Umgab das liebliche Gesicht,
Und Zärtlichkeit für mich - ihr Götter!
Ich hofft es, ich verdient es nicht!

Doch ach, schon mit der Morgensonne
Verengt der Abschied mir das Herz:
In deinen Küssen welche Wonne!
In deinem Auge welcher Schmerz!
Ich ging, du standst und sahst zur Erden
Und sahst mir nach mit nassem Blick:
Und doch, welch Glück, geliebt zu werden!
Und lieben, Götter, welch ein Glück!

WELCOME AND FAREWELL

My heart beat fast: to horse! away!
No sooner thought than it was done.
The evening held earth in its sway,
And night upon the mountains hung.
Shrouded in mist there stood the oak,
A giant of colossal size,
While darkness pierced the undergrowth
With myriad atramentous eyes.

Behind a clouded hill the moon
Endeavoured timidly to peer;
On wings of whispered song, the breeze
Played eerily about my ear;
Night spawned a thousand monsters there,
Yet blithe in spirit on I pressed:
Within my veins what glowing fire!
What burning ardour in my breast!

I saw you, and such tender joy
Flowed from your sweet gaze to my own;
My heart was wholly at your side,
Each breath I took for you alone.
A gentle shade of vernal rose
Upon your features I observed;
Such tenderness for me — ye gods!
So hoped for yet so undeserved!

But with the morning sun's first light
Adieu's sweet sorrow gripped my heart:
In those last kisses what delight!
In those fair eyes what bitter smart!
I left. You stood with eyes downcast
In tears your heart could not suppress:
And yet, what joy it is to love!
And to be loved, ye gods, what bliss!

ERLKÖNIG

Wer reitet so spät durch Nacht und Wind?
Es ist der Vater mit seinem Kind;
Er hat den Knaben wohl in dem Arm,
Er faßt ihn sicher, er hält ihn warm.

Mein Sohn, was birgst du so bang dein Gesicht?
Siehst, Vater, du den Erlkönig nicht?
Den Erlenkönig mit Kron' und Schweif?
Mein Sohn, es ist ein Nebelstreif.

"Du liebes Kind, komm, geh mit mir!
Gar schöne Spiele spiel' ich mit dir;
Manch' bunte Blumen sind an dem Strand,
Meine Mutter hat manch gülden Gewand."

Mein Vater, mein Vater, und hörest du nicht,
Was Erlenkönig mir leise verspricht?
Sei ruhig, bleibe ruhig, mein Kind;
In dürren Blättern säuselt der Wind.

"Willst, feiner Knabe, du mit mir gehn?
Meine Töchter sollen dich warten schön;
Meine Töchter führen den nächtlichen Reihn,
Und wiegen und tanzen und singen dich ein."

Mein Vater, mein Vater, und siehst du nicht dort
Erlkönigs Töchter am düstern Ort?
Mein Sohn, mein Sohn, ich seh' es genau:
Es scheinen die alten Weiden so grau.

"Ich liebe dich, mich reizt deine schöne Gestalt;
Und bist du nicht willig, so brauch' ich Gewalt."
Mein Vater, mein Vater, jetzt faßt er mich an!
Erlkönig hat mir ein Leids getan!

Dem Vater grauset's; er reitet geschwind,
Er hält in den Armen das ächzende Kind,
Erreicht den Hof mit Mühe und Not;
In seinen Armen, das Kind war tot.

THE ELF KING

Who rides so late through the night so wild?
It is the father with his child;
He clasps the boy fast in his arm,
To keep him warm and free from harm.

My son, why hide you your face in fear?
See you not, father, the Elf King here,
The Elf King with his train and crown?
My son, 'tis mist upon the down.

"My darling child, come stay with me!
Such wondrous games I'll play with thee,
Such fragrant flow'rs grow on the wold,
My mother wears a robe of gold."

My father, my father, do you not hear
What Elf King whispers in my ear?
Be calm, my child, you need not fear,
'Tis but the rustling leaves you hear.

"My handsome boy, wilt thou come with me?
My daughters are ready to wait on thee;
My daughters their nightly vigil will keep —
Their singing and dancing will lull thee to sleep."

My father, my father, see you not there
The Elf King's daughters in their sombre lair?
My son, my son, all that I discern
Are the old grey willows and the dancing fern.

"I love thee child, thy form doth arouse my delight;
And art thou not willing, I'll take thee by might!"
My father, my father, he's grasping my arm,
Elf King has done me a dreadful harm!

Fear grips the father; he speeds through the wild;
He holds to his bosom the shuddering child;
He reaches the courtyard in anguish and dread;
In his arms, the child lay dead.

'Lamartine's Cave'. The setting for his poem 'The Lake'
Publicity poster for the French Railways, 1927

ALPHONSE DE LAMARTINE (1790-1869)

Photograph by Félix Nadar, 1856

L'ISOLEMENT

Souvent sur la montagne, à l'ombre du vieux chêne,
Au coucher du soleil, tristement je m'assieds ;
Je promène au hasard mes regards sur la plaine,
Dont le tableau changeant se déroule à mes pieds.

Ici gronde le fleuve aux vagues écumantes ;
Il serpente, et s'enfonce en un lointain obscur ;
Là le lac immobile étend ses eaux dormantes
Où l'étoile du soir se lève dans l'azur.

Au sommet de ces monts couronnés de bois sombres,
Le crépuscule encor jette un dernier rayon ;
Et le char vaporeux de la reine des ombres
Monte, et blanchit déjà les bords de l'horizon.

Cependant, s'élançant de la flèche gothique,
Un son religieux se répand dans les airs :
Le voyageur s'arrête, et la cloche rustique
Aux derniers bruits du jour mêle de saints concerts.

Mais à ces doux tableaux mon âme indifférente
N'éprouve devant eux ni charme ni transports ;
Je contemple la terre ainsi qu'une ombre errante
Le soleil des vivants n'échauffe plus les morts.

De colline en colline en vain portant ma vue,
u sud à l'aquilon, de l'aurore au couchant,
Je parcours tous les points de l'immense étendue,
Et je dis : " Nulle part le bonheur ne m'attend. "

Que me font ces vallons, ces palais, ces chaumières,
Vains objets dont pour moi le charme est envolé ?
Fleuves, rochers, forêts, solitudes si chères,
Un seul être vous manque, et tout est dépeuplé !

Que le tour du soleil ou commence ou s'achève,
D'un oeil indifférent je le suis dans son cours ;
En un ciel sombre ou pur qu'il se couche ou se lève,
Qu'importe le soleil ? je n'attends rien des jours.

SOLITUDE

Often, up on the hillside, in the old oak's shade,
I sit, wistfully pensive, in the late evening's glow;
Across the open plain o'er which my eyes have strayed,
An ever-changing vista stretches out below.

Here, the tumultuous river's foaming billows break;
Meandering, it sinks into the gloom afar;
There, motionless, the dormant waters of the lake
Reflect in the azure the rising evening star.

Upon the mountain's crest, crowned by a sombre wood,
A final glimmer in the twilight grows more dim,
And the ethereal chariot of the queen of shade
Ascends, and renders pale the skyline's tranquil rim.

Meanwhile, issuing forth from a mediaeval spire,
The sound of sacred music permeates the air,
The wayfarer takes pause, and the old rustic bell
Blends with the day's last sounds its saintly, solemn air.

But my soul is not moved by these harmonious scenes
That on my listless soul no charm or joy can shed;
Like a wandering shadow I contemplate the earth:
The sun of living souls no longer warms the dead.

From hill to hill in vain I turn my restless gaze;
From south to north, from daybreak to the setting sun,
My eyes scan every part of the immense expanse,
And I think: "Nowhere here can sorrow be undone."

What good to me are valleys, mansions, cottages,
Vain objects for whose beauty I no longer care?
Beloved solitude of forests, rivers, rocks,
One mortal soul is absent, and all is barren there.

Whether the sun begins or ends its daily course,
I follow its migration with an indifferent gaze;
Whether it sets or rises in bright or sombre skies,
What care I for the sun? I weary of my days.

L'ISOLEMENT

Quand je pourrais le suivre en sa vaste carrière,
Mes yeux verraient partout le vide et les déserts :
Je ne désire rien de tout ce qu'il éclaire ;
Je ne demande rien à l'immense univers.

Mais peut-être au-delà des bornes de sa sphère,
Lieux où le vrai soleil éclaire d'autres cieux,
Si je pouvais laisser ma dépouille à la terre,
Ce que j'ai tant rêvé paraîtrait à mes yeux !

Là, je m'enivrerais à la source où j'aspire ;
Là, je retrouverais et l'espoir et l'amour,
Et ce bien idéal que toute âme désire,
Et qui n'a pas de nom au terrestre séjour !

Que ne puîs-je, porté sur le char de l'Aurore,
Vague objet de mes vœux, m'élancer jusqu'à toi !
Sur la terre d'exil pourquoi resté-je encore ?
Il n'est rien de commun entre la terre et moi.

Quand la feuille des bois tombe dans la prairie,
Le vent du soir s'élève et l'arrache aux vallons ;
Et moi, je suis semblable à la feuille flétrie :
Emportez-moi comme elle, orageux aquilons !

SOLITUDE

If I could follow it in its relentless run,
My eyes would only see deserted, barren land;
I wish for nothing that's illumined by the sun,
On all of vast creation I make no demand.

And yet perhaps beyond the limits of its sphere,
In places where the true sun lights up other skies,
If only I could leave my body to the earth,
What I have dreamed of would appear before my eyes!

There, I would grow drunk at the spring for which I yearn;
There, I would find once more both hope and love again,
And that ideal estate which every soul desires,
That has no name while we sojourn in earth's domain.

If I could only, on Aurora's chariot,
Vague object of my fancy, be transported to thee!
Why do I still remain in exile on the earth?
There is no harmony between the earth and me.

The withered autumn leaf that lies upon the heath
Is snatched from whence it fell and borne away upon
A gust of evening wind; I am a withered leaf:
O take me with you too, unbridled aquilon!

LE LAC

Ainsi, toujours poussés vers de nouveaux rivages,
Dans la nuit éternelle emportés sans retour,
Ne pourrons-nous jamais sur l'océan des âges
Jeter l'ancre un seul jour ?

Ô lac ! l'année à peine a fini sa carrière,
Et près des flots chéris qu'elle devait revoir,
Regarde ! je viens seul m'asseoir sur cette pierre
Où tu la vis s'asseoir !

Tu mugissais ainsi sous ces roches profondes,
Ainsi tu te brisais sur leurs flancs déchirés,
Ainsi le vent jetait l'écume de tes ondes
Sur ses pieds adorés.

Un soir, t'en souvient-il ? nous voguions en silence ;
On n'entendait au loin, sur l'onde et sous les cieux,
Que le bruit des rameurs qui frappaient en cadence
Tes flots harmonieux.

Tout à coup des accents inconnus à la terre
Du rivage charmé frappèrent les échos ;
Le flot fut attentif, et la voix qui m'est chère
Laissa tomber ces mots :

« Ô temps ! suspends ton vol, et vous, heures propices !
Suspendez votre cours :
Laissez-nous savourer les rapides délices
Des plus beaux de nos jours !

« Assez de malheureux ici-bas vous implorent,
Coulez, coulez pour eux ;
Prenez avec leurs jours les soins qui les dévorent ;
Oubliez les heureux.

THE LAKE

Thus, carried ever forth to undiscovered shores,
Into eternal night forever borne away,
Can we not once upon the vast ocean of time
Drop anchor for a day?

Oh lake, the present year has scarcely run its course,
By cherished waves that she ought once more to have seen,
Look! I have come alone to sit on this rock where
She used to sit and dream!

Thus did your waters roar beneath these lofty cliffs,
Against their rugged flanks your surging billows beat,
While gusts of wind dispersed the lather of their spray
On her beloved feet.

One night, do you recall? we drifted silently;
Afloat beneath the lake's celestial canopy,
With just the sound of oars that skimmed the tranquil deep
In rhythmic harmony.

All of a sudden, accents unknown to the earth
From your enchanted shore echoed imploringly;
Your waters lent their ear, and that beloved voice
Let fall this fervent plea:

"O Time! Suspend your flight, and you, propitious hours,
Suspend your daily race!
Let us have pause to taste the transient delights
Of our most happy days!

"So many wretched souls here on this earth implore;
Receive them in your flow;
Take with their days the pain and anguish they endure;
Let the happy go.

LE LAC

« Mais je demande en vain quelques moments encore,
Le temps m'échappe et fuit ;
Je dis à cette nuit : Sois plus lente ; et l'aurore
Va dissiper la nuit.

« Aimons donc, aimons donc ! de l'heure fugitive,
Hâtons-nous, jouissons !
L'homme n'a point de port, le temps n'a point de rive ;
Il coule, et nous passons ! »

Temps jaloux, se peut-il que ces moments d'ivresse,
Où l'amour à longs flots nous verse le bonheur,
S'envolent loin de nous de la même vitesse
Que les jours de malheur ?

Eh quoi ! n'en pourrons-nous fixer au moins la trace ?
Quoi ! passés pour jamais ! quoi ! tout entiers perdus !
Ce temps qui les donna, ce temps qui les efface,
Ne nous les rendra plus !

Éternité, néant, passé, sombres abîmes,
Que faites-vous des jours que vous engloutissez ?
Parlez : nous rendrez-vous ces extases sublimes
Que vous nous ravissez ?

Ô lac ! rochers muets ! grottes ! forêt obscure !
Vous, que le temps épargne ou qu'il peut rajeunir,
Gardez de cette nuit, gardez, belle nature,
Au moins le souvenir !

Qu'il soit dans ton repos, qu'il soit dans tes orages,
Beau lac, et dans l'aspect de tes riants coteaux,
Et dans ces noirs sapins, et dans ces rocs sauvages
Qui pendent sur tes eaux.

THE LAKE

"But I request in vain those moments to retain;
Time shuns me in its flight;
I say unto the night: Slow down! and yet the dawn
Will dissipate the night.

"Therefore let's love, let's love! Let's hasten to enjoy
The hour that soon is gone!
Man has no port of call, for time there is no shore!
It flows, and we pass on!"

Harsh time, how can it be that moments of sweet bliss,
When love pours from its urn great floods of happiness,
Can take their leave from us so much more rapidly
Than days of wretchedness?

What! Can we then not fix at least a trace of it?
What! Gone forever! What! Does nothing now remain?
Those moments granted us, those moments now erased,
Will not return again!

Eternity, past time, dark chasms, nothingness,
What do you with the days that you have swallowed up?
Speak! Will you give us back those ecstasies sublime
That you have snatched from us?

O Lake, your silent rocks, your grottos, your dark woods,
You, whom time spares or even can rejuvenate,
Fair Nature, will you keep at least the memory
Of this enchanted night!

Be it in your repose or in your raging storms,
Fair Lake, and in the joy of laughing hillsides, and
In these dark pine trees, and in these primeval rocks
That o'er your waters stand;

LE LAC

Qu'il soit dans le zéphyr qui frémit et qui passe,
dans les bruits de tes bords par tes bords répétés,
dans l'astre au front d'argent qui blanchit ta surface
de ses molles clartés.

Que le vent qui gémit, le roseau qui soupire
que les parfums légers de ton air embaumé,
que tout ce qu'on entend, l'on voit ou l'on respire,
tout dise: Ils ont aimé!

THE LAKE

Be it in gentle winds that tremble as they pass,
In sounds that from your banks ring out from shore to shore,
Or in the silver glow of stars that on your waters
Their gentle radiance pour.

May the lamenting winds, the sighing of the reeds,
The balmy breeze that wafts its fragrance from above,
May everything we see, and hear, and live, and breathe,
All say: here they did love!

Victor Hugo writing with a quill pen during a session of the Académie française. Ink drawing by Prosper Mérimée, ca. 1845-1850

Caricature of Victor Hugo by Honoré Daumier, 1849

VICTOR HUGO (1802 – 1885)

Photograph by Étienne Carjat, 1876

Demain, dès l'aube, à l'heure où blanchit la campagne,
Je partirai. Vois-tu, je sais que tu m'attends.
J'irai par la forêt, j'irai par la montagne.
Je ne puis demeurer loin de toi plus longtemps.

Je marcherai les yeux fixés sur mes pensées,
Sans rien voir au dehors, sans entendre aucun bruit,
Seul, inconnu, le dos courbé, les mains croisées,
Triste, et le jour pour moi sera comme la nuit.

Je ne regarderai ni l'or du soir qui tombe,
Ni les voiles au loin descendant vers Harfleur,
Et quand j'arriverai, je mettrai sur ta tombe
Un bouquet de houx vert et de bruyère en fleur.

Tomorrow, when the dawn whitens the countryside,
I shall depart. I know that you await me too;
I'll traverse wood and field, valley and mountainside.
No longer can I bear to be apart from you.

In silence I shall walk, my ears immune to sound,
My eyes fixed on my thoughts, impervious to the light,
Alone, unrecognised, head bowed toward the ground
In sadness, and the day for me will be like night.

I shall not pause to gaze on evening's golden grace,
Nor watch the distant sails descending on Harfleur,
And then, when I arrive, upon your grave I'll place
A wreath of holly green and flowering heather there.

L'aube est moins claire, l'air moins chaud, le ciel moins pur ;
Le soir brumeux ternit les astres de l'azur.
Les longs jours sont passés ; les mois charmants finissent.
Hélas ! voici déjà les arbres qui jaunissent !
Comme le temps s'en va d'un pas précipité !
Il semble que nos yeux, qu'éblouissait l'été,
Ont à peine eu le temps de voir les feuilles vertes.

Pour qui vit comme moi les fenêtres ouvertes,
L'automne est triste avec sa bise et son brouillard,
Et l'été qui s'enfuit est un ami qui part.
Adieu, dit cette voix qui dans notre âme pleure,
Adieu, ciel bleu ! beau ciel qu'un souffle tiède effleure !
Voluptés du grand air, bruit d'ailes dans les bois,
Promenades, ravins pleins de lointaines voix,
Fleurs, bonheur innocent des âmes apaisées,
Adieu, rayonnements ! aubes ! chansons ! rosées !

Puis tout bas on ajoute : ô jours bénis et doux !
Hélas ! vous reviendrez ! me retrouverez-vous ?

Dawn is less clear, the air less warm, the sky less pure;
An evening mist now veils the stars of the azure.
The long days are no more; the months so warm and mellow
Have flown, alas! See how the trees are turning yellow!
How time pursues its course at such a frenzied pace!
It would seem that our eyes, dazzled by summer's race,
Have barely caught a glimpse of verdant countryside.

For those of us who love to throw our windows wide,
Autumn brings only sorrow, as the mists descend,
And summer takes its leave like a departing friend.
Farewell! laments the voice that weeps within the breast!
Farewell, clear azure skies by gentle winds caressed!
Joys of the great outdoors, birds winging in the dene,
Excursions, voices heard from deep in the ravine,
Flow'rs, innocent delights of souls refreshed anew,
Farewell, aurora's glow! songs! sunlight! morning dew!

Then, quietly, we ask: O blest days of the year!
Alas! you will return! Will you still find me here?

OCEANO NOX

Oh ! combien de marins, combien de capitaines
Qui sont partis joyeux pour des courses lointaines,
Dans ce morne horizon se sont évanouis !
Combien ont disparu, dure et triste fortune !
Dans une mer sans fond, par une nuit sans lune,
Sous l'aveugle océan à jamais enfouis !

Combien de patrons morts avec leurs équipages !
L'ouragan de leur vie a pris toutes les pages
Et d'un souffle il a tout dispersé sur les flots !
Nul ne saura leur fin dans l'abîme plongée.
Chaque vague en passant d'un butin s'est chargée ;
L'une a saisi l'esquif, l'autre les matelots !

Nul ne sait votre sort, pauvres têtes perdues !
Vous roulez à travers les sombres étendues,
Heurtant de vos fronts morts des écueils inconnus.
Oh ! que de vieux parents, qui n'avaient plus qu'un rêve,
Sont morts en attendant tous les jours sur la grève
Ceux qui ne sont pas revenus !

On s'entretient de vous parfois dans les veillées.
Maint joyeux cercle, assis sur des ancres rouillées,
Mêle encor quelque temps vos noms d'ombre couverts
Aux rires, aux refrains, aux récits d'aventures,
Aux baisers qu'on dérobe à vos belles futures,
Tandis que vous dormez dans les goémons verts !

On demande : - Où sont-ils ? sont-ils rois dans quelque île ?
Nous ont-ils délaissés pour un bord plus fertile ? -
Puis votre souvenir même est enseveli.
Le corps se perd dans l'eau, le nom dans la mémoire.
Le temps, qui sur toute ombre en verse une plus noire,
Sur le sombre océan jette le sombre oubli.

OCEANO NOX

Oh! How many seafarers, captains and their crew
Who set out full of joy in search of something new,
Upon the bleak horizon have vanished without trace!
How many souls have found, O cruel destiny!
On a dark moonless night, on an unfathomed sea,
Beneath the sombre waves, their final resting place!

How many ship's commanders perished with their crew!
The storm took every page of the life they once knew
And in one breath across the billows scattered them.
No one can know their end, plunged into the abyss.
Each passing wave laid claim to its share of the prize,
One grabbed hold of the ship, the other seized the men.

Nobody knows your fate, poor heads lost in the lave
Of the dark ocean, tossed about from wave to wave,
Your dead brows striking reefs that hide beneath the churn.
How many parents, clinging to a dream, have died,
Waiting from day to day down at the harbourside
For those who never will return!

Sometimes late in the day they sit and speak of you.
Seated on rusty anchors, many a jovial crew
Still mingle for a while your names, lost in the black
Morass of time, with tales of exploits, merry song,
And kisses shared with beauty that to you did once belong,
While you lie sleeping in your bed of green sea wrack!

They ask: — Where are they now? Are they kings on some isle?
Did they desert us for lands that are more fertile? —
But then the very thought of you no more abides.
Your body's lost to water, your name to memory.
And time, which on the gloom pours more obscurity,
Casts dark oblivion upon the mournful tides.

OCEANO NOX

Bientôt des yeux de tous votre ombre est disparue.
L'un n'a-t-il pas sa barque et l'autre sa charrue ?
Seules, durant ces nuits où l'orage est vainqueur,
Vos veuves aux fronts blancs, lasses de vous attendre,
Parlent encor de vous en remuant la cendre
De leur foyer et de leur cœur !

Et quand la tombe enfin a fermé leur paupière,
Rien ne sait plus vos noms, pas même une humble pierre
Dans l'étroit cimetière où l'écho nous répond,
Pas même un saule vert qui s'effeuille à l'automne,
Pas même la chanson naïve et monotone
Que chante un mendiant à l'angle d'un vieux pont !

Où sont-ils, les marins sombrés dans les nuits noires ?
O flots, que vous savez de lugubres histoires !
Flots profonds redoutés des mères à genoux !
Vous vous les racontez en montant les marées,
Et c'est ce qui vous fait ces voix désespérées
Que vous avez le soir quand vous venez vers nous !

OCEANO NOX

Your shadow from the eyes of all has vanished now.
Does one not have his boat, and the other his plough?
Alone, during those nights when raging tempests start,
Your pale-browed widows, wearied by their endless wait,
Still speak of you as they turn over in the grate
The ashes of their home and heart!

And when at last they too lie in the tomb, alone,
Nothing will know your names, not even the old stone
In the small cemetery where silence echoes long,
Not even the green tree that sheds its foliage,
Not even, at the corner of an ancient bridge,
The droning monotone of an old beggar's song!

Where are they now, those men, plunged into stygian seas?
O billows, you must know such doleful histories!
Great billows, feared by mothers as they kneel to pray!
You share them with each other as you break against the shore,
And that is why we hear that long despairing roar
When in the night your mournful echoes come our way!

L'EXPIATION

I

Il neigeait. On était vaincu par sa conquête.
Pour la première fois l'aigle baissait la tête.
Sombres jours ! l'empereur revenait lentement,
Laissant derrière lui brûler Moscou fumant.
Il neigeait. L'âpre hiver fondait en avalanche.
Après la plaine blanche une autre plaine blanche.
On ne connaissait plus les chefs ni le drapeau.
Hier la grande armée, et maintenant troupeau.
On ne distinguait plus les ailes ni le centre.
Il neigeait. Les blessés s'abritaient dans le ventre
Des chevaux morts ; au seuil des bivouacs désolés
On voyait des clairons à leur poste gelés,
Restés debout, en selle et muets, blancs de givre,
Collant leur bouche en pierre aux trompettes de cuivre.
Boulets, mitraille, obus, mêlés aux flocons blancs,
Pleuvaient ; les grenadiers, surpris d'être tremblants,
Marchaient pensifs, la glace à leur moustache grise.
Il neigeait, il neigeait toujours! La froide bise
Sifflait ; sur le verglas, dans des lieux inconnus,
On n'avait pas de pain et l'on allait pieds nus.
Ce n'étaient plus des cœurs vivants, des gens de guerre :
C'était un rêve errant dans la brume, un mystère,
Une procession d'ombres sous le ciel noir.
La solitude vaste, épouvantable à voir,
Partout apparaissait, muette vengeresse.
Le ciel faisait sans bruit avec la neige épaisse
Pour cette immense armée un immense linceul.
Et, chacun se sentant mourir, on était seul.
– Sortira-t-on jamais de ce funeste empire ?
Deux ennemis ! le czar, le nord. Le nord est pire.
On jetait les canons pour brûler les affûts.
Qui se couchait, mourait. Groupe morne et confus,
Ils fuyaient ; le désert dévorait le cortège.
On pouvait, à des plis qui soulevaient la neige,
Voir que des régiments s'étaient endormis là.

ATONEMENT

I

It snowed. Victory had brought failure in its stead,
Alas! For the first time, the eagle bowed its head.
The emperor retreated slowly, — sombre days!
Leaving behind him smoking Moscow, still ablaze.
It snowed. Harsh winter had released an avalanche.
Beyond the white expanse another white expanse.
Commander, infantry, and standard, all were blurred.
The grand army of yesterday was now a herd.
Both flank and centre could no longer be descried.
It snowed. The wounded men were sheltering inside
Dead horses' bellies; near bleak bivouacs, like ghosts,
Petrified trumpeters stood frozen to their posts,
Stiff in the saddle, white with frost, silent, alone,
Their silver trumpets welded to their lips of stone.
Cannonballs, grapeshot, shells, with flakes of snow entwined,
Rained down; the grenadiers, who were surprised to find
They trembled, journeyed on, their grey beards stiff with frost.
It snowed, again it snowed! The wind whistled across
The desolate terrain; they had no bread to eat,
And on the freezing ground no boots to warm their feet.
No longer warriors brave of horse or infantry,
They were now but a dream lost in a mystery,
A cavalcade of shadows beneath a stygian sky.
The boundless solitude, appalling to the eye,
In silent retribution reigned o'er the frozen ground.
The sky, opaque with snow, without even a sound,
Became for that great army one enormous shroud,
And each foresaw his death beneath that sombre cloud.
– Will they never escape this baleful empire's curse?
Two enemies! the tsar, the north. The north is worse.
The wooden carts were stripped of cannon to make fire.
Who lay down, died. The rest fled in confusion dire;
The wilderness was feeding on the convoy there.
In the protruding folds of snow you could see where
Entire battalions as if in slumber lay.

L'EXPIATION

Ô chutes d'Annibal ! lendemains d'Attila !
Fuyards, blessés, mourants, caissons, brancards, civières,
On s'écrasait aux ponts pour passer les rivières,
On s'endormait dix mille, on se réveillait cent.
Ney, que suivait naguère une armée, à présent
S'évadait, disputant sa montre à trois cosaques.
Toutes les nuits, qui vive ! alerte, assauts ! attaques !
Ces fantômes prenaient leur fusil, et sur eux
Ils voyaient se ruer, effrayants, ténébreux,
Avec des cris pareils aux voix des vautours chauves,
D'horribles escadrons, tourbillons d'hommes fauves.
Toute une armée ainsi dans la nuit se perdait.
L'empereur était là, debout, qui regardait.
Il était comme un arbre en proie à la cognée.
Sur ce géant, grandeur jusqu'alors épargnée,
Le malheur, bûcheron sinistre, était monté ;
Et lui, chêne vivant, par la hache insulté,
Tressaillant sous le spectre aux lugubres revanches,
Il regardait tomber autour de lui ses branches.
Chefs, soldats, tous mouraient. Chacun avait son tour.
Tandis qu'environnant sa tente avec amour,
Voyant son ombre aller et venir sur la toile,
Ceux qui restaient, croyant toujours à son étoile,
Accusaient le destin de lèse-majesté,
Lui se sentit soudain dans l'âme épouvanté.
Stupéfait du désastre et ne sachant que croire,
L'empereur se tourna vers Dieu ; l'homme de gloire
Trembla ; Napoléon comprit qu'il expiait
Quelque chose peut-être, et, livide, inquiet,
Devant ses légions sur la neige semées :
« Est-ce le châtiment, dit-il. Dieu des armées ? »
Alors il s'entendit appeler par son nom
Et quelqu'un qui parlait dans l'ombre lui dit : Non.

ATONEMENT

O fall of Hannibal! Attila's fateful day!
Strongboxes, stretchers, casks, the wounded and the dead,
Crammed bridges when the rivers blocked the way ahead.
Ten thousand fell asleep, a hundred woke next day.
He who had led victorious armies, Marshal Ney,
Took flight, bartering for his watch with three Cossacks.
And every night, qui vive! Alerts, assaults! attacks!
Those phantoms gathered up their weapons, and they saw
Rushing towards them in the darkness, striking awe,
Shrieking like vultures, charging time and time again,
Fearsome battalions, whirlwinds of savage men.
A whole army was lost during a single night.
The emperor was there, watching their woeful plight.
He stood there like a tree that's for the axe prepared.
Upon this giant's greatness, that till then had been spared,
Misfortune, evil woodman; had mounted fierce attacks,
And he, a living oak, insulted by the axe,
Cowed by the sombre vengeance that he could foretell,
Watched, trembling, as around him all his branches fell.
Officers, soldiers, all were killed, each in his turn.
While round his tent, with love that constantly would burn,
Seeing his shadow on the canvas come and go,
Those who remained, still sure his star would ever glow,
Accused harsh destiny of lèse-majesté,
While he felt his soul gripped by dire anxiety.
Not knowing what to think, by disaster downtrod,
The emperor, erstwhile victorious, turned to God,
Trembling; Napoleon knew that he must atone
Perhaps for something, and, pale, anxious and alone,
Before his legions scattered all across the snow:
"O God, is this the punishment that you bestow?"
Whereon he heard a voice that spoke his name, and lo!
Out of the realms of darkness came the answer: No.

L'EXPIATION

II

Waterloo ! Waterloo ! Waterloo ! morne plaine !
Comme une onde qui bout dans une urne trop pleine,
Dans ton cirque de bois, de coteaux, de vallons,
La pâle mort mêlait les sombres bataillons.
D'un côté c'est l'Europe et de l'autre la France.
Choc sanglant ! des héros Dieu trompait l'espérance ;
Tu désertais, victoire, et le sort était las.
O Waterloo ! je pleure et je m'arrête, hélas !
Car ces derniers soldats de la dernière guerre
Furent grands ; ils avaient vaincu toute la terre,
Chassé vingt rois, passé les Alpes et le Rhin,
Et leur âme chantait dans les clairons d'airain !

Le soir tombait ; la lutte était ardente et noire.
Il avait l'offensive et presque la victoire ;
Il tenait Wellington acculé sur un bois.
Sa lunette à la main, il observait parfois
Le centre du combat, point obscur où tressaille
La mêlée, effroyable et vivante broussaille,
Et parfois l'horizon, sombre comme la mer.
Soudain, joyeux, il dit : Grouchy ! – C'était Blücher.
L'espoir changea de camp, le combat changea d'âme,
La mêlée en hurlant grandit comme une flamme.
La batterie anglaise écrasa nos carrés.
La plaine, où frissonnaient les drapeaux déchirés,
Ne fut plus, dans les cris des mourants qu'on égorge,
Qu'un gouffre flamboyant, rouge comme une forge ;
Gouffre où les régiments comme des pans de murs
Tombaient, où se couchaient comme des épis mûrs
Les hauts tambours-majors aux panaches énormes,
Où l'on entrevoyait des blessures difformes !
Carnage affreux ! moment fatal ! L'homme inquiet
Sentit que la bataille entre ses mains pliait.
Derrière un mamelon la garde était massée.
La garde, espoir suprême et suprême pensée !

ATONEMENT

II

Waterloo! Waterloo! Waterloo! dismal field!
Like water boiling in an urn that's overfilled,
Within your arc of woods and valleys, the last breath
Of grim battalions engaged with pallid death.
On one side Europe stood, the other side France trod.
A bloody clash! The hope of heroes dashed by God;
Victory, you took flight and destiny was weak.
O Waterloo, alas! I am resigned to weep!
For those old combatants who fought in former wars
Were great; of the whole world they were the conquerors,
They drove out twenty kings, the Alps and Rhine they passed,
And their brave spirit sang in clarions of brass!

Night fell; the battle fiercely raged; the sky was black.
Victory beckoned as he boosted the attack;
He had Wellington cornered hard against a wood.
His eyeglass in his hand, he watched, sometimes he could
Discern the centre of the fray where quaked a rush
Of bodies, fearsome horde of living human brush,
And sometimes the horizon, sombre as the sea.
Suddenly, jubilant, he cried: it is Grouchy!
– It was Blücher. Hope changed camp, and the fight its soul,
The howling melee grew like wildfire, and the whole
Of England's cannonry down on our squares did rain;
Our lacerated standards fluttered on the plain
That had become, strewn with the dying and the dead,
A fiery blazing gulf, a forge of vibrant red.
A gulf where regiments fell like a crumbling wall,
Where men, like ears of ripened corn were seen to fall;
Drum-majors, whose great plumes lay strewn across the ground,
Displayed for all to see their hideous open wounds!
Dire carnage! fatal moment! Anxious, there he stands,
Sensing that the campaign was crumbling in his hands.
Behind a mound the Guard was massed upon a slope.
The Guard, supreme last thought! supreme and only hope!

L'EXPIATION

« Allons ! faites donner la garde ! » cria-t-il.
Et, lanciers, grenadiers aux guêtres de coutil,
Dragons que Rome eût pris pour des légionnaires,
Cuirassiers, canonniers qui traînaient des tonnerres,
Portant le noir colback ou le casque poli,
Tous, ceux de Friedland et ceux de Rivoli,
Comprenant qu'ils allaient mourir dans cette fête,
Saluèrent leur dieu, debout dans la tempête.
Leur bouche, d'un seul cri, dit : vive l'empereur !
Puis, à pas lents, musique en tête, sans fureur,
Tranquille, souriant à la mitraille anglaise,
La garde impériale entra dans la fournaise.
Hélas ! Napoléon, sur sa garde penché,
Regardait, et, sitôt qu'ils avaient débouché
Sous les sombres canons crachant des jets de soufre,
Voyait, l'un après l'autre, en cet horrible gouffre,
Fondre ces régiments de granit et d'acier
Comme fond une cire au souffle d'un brasier.
Ils allaient, l'arme au bras, front haut, graves, stoïques.
Pas un ne recula. Dormez, morts héroïques !
Le reste de l'armée hésitait sur leurs corps
Et regardait mourir la garde. – C'est alors
Qu'élevant tout à coup sa voix désespérée,
La Déroute, géante à la face effarée
Qui, pâle, épouvantant les plus fiers bataillons,
Changeant subitement les drapeaux en haillons,
A de certains moments, spectre fait de fumées,
Se lève grandissante au milieu des armées,
La Déroute apparut au soldat qui s'émeut,
Et, se tordant les bras, cria : Sauve qui peut !
Sauve qui peut ! – affront ! horreur ! – toutes les bouches
Criaient ; à travers champs, fous, éperdus, farouches,
Comme si quelque souffle avait passé sur eux.
Parmi les lourds caissons et les fourgons poudreux,
Roulant dans les fossés, se cachant dans les seigles,
Jetant shakos, manteaux, fusils, jetant les aigles.

ATONEMENT

"Come on! Send in the Guard! send in the Guard!" he cried.
And lancers, grenadiers with gaiters made of hide,
Dragoons Rome would have taken to be legionnaires,
Thunderous cannons dragged by gunners, cuirassiers,
Wearing the black colback or polished helmetry,
The men of Friedland, Austerlitz and Rivoli,
Knowing they were to die, into this feast they trod,
Into the raging storm, acknowledging their god.
"Long live the emperor!" they cried in unison.
Then, as the bandsmen played, a full battalion
Of the Imperial Guard, slowly making their way,
Smiling at English guns, calmly entered the fray.
Alas! Napoleon, the Guard his only hope,
Was watching closely as the men their cover broke
Just as the guns unleashed a veritable blitz
Of grapeshot, and he saw, in that dreadful abyss,
Whole regiments of steel and granite melt away
Like wax beneath a flaming torch that fateful day.
They went, arms sloped, austere, stoic, with unbowed head,
Not one of them turned back. Sleep sound, heroic dead!
The rest of the army held their positions hard
And watched in silence the destruction of the Guard.
Then, in despairing tones that filled the open space,
The Rout appeared, a giant with horror on her face;
Her pallor filled the proudest regiments with dread.
Suddenly tearing every standard to a shred,
Increasing hour by hour, the spectre, wreathed in smoke,
Coming to spread despair amid the armies, spoke,
Making the bravest men begin to doubt the strife.
Wringing her hands, the Rout then cried: Run for your life!
Run for your life! affront! horror! –Their cries were fraught
With terror; across fields they fled, wild-eyed, distraught,
As if sustained in motion by a sudden gust
Of wind. Amid the crates and carts, laden with dust,
They scrambled into ditches or fields of corn to hide,
Their helmets, greatcoats, guns, and eagles cast aside.

L'EXPIATION

Sous les sabres prussiens, ces vétérans, ô deuil !
Tremblaient, hurlaient, pleuraient, couraient ! – En un clin d'œil,
Comme s'envole au vent une paille enflammée,
S'évanouit ce bruit qui fut la grande armée,
Et cette plaine, hélas, où l'on rêve aujourd'hui,
Vit fuir ceux devant qui l'univers avait fui !
Quarante ans sont passés, et ce coin de la terre,
Waterloo, ce plateau funèbre et solitaire,
Ce champ sinistre où Dieu mêla tant de néants,
Tremble encor d'avoir vu la fuite des géants !

Napoléon les vit s'écouler comme un fleuve ;
Hommes, chevaux, tambours, drapeaux ; – et dans l'épreuve
Sentant confusément revenir son remords,
Levant les mains au ciel, il dit : « Mes soldats morts,
Moi vaincu ! mon empire est brisé comme verre.
Est-ce le châtiment cette fois, Dieu sévère ? »
Alors parmi les cris, les rumeurs, le canon,
Il entendit la voix qui lui répondait : Non !

ATONEMENT

Beneath the Prussian swords, those veterans, o grief!
Ran trembling, weeping, howling in their disbelief,
And like a burning straw on zephyr breezes blown,
The roar of the Great Army had vanished and was gone,
And that vast plain, alas, of which we dream today,
Saw fleeing those from whom the whole world fled away!
This corner of the earth, now forty years have passed,
Waterloo, this plateau, austere and overcast,
This sombre field, on which God wrought eternal night,
Still trembles to have seen those giants in their flight!

Napoleon saw them retreating in a flood
Of soldiers, horses, drums, and standards, as he stood,
Confused, sensing remorse returning, and he said,
Raising his hands to heaven: "My soldiers are all dead,
And I'm defeated, my empire a shattered glass!
Unyielding God, is this the punishment at last?
Amid the noise of guns, the shouts, the cries of woe,
He heard again the voice, and that voice answered: No!

Charles Baudelaire
Self-portrait under the influence of hashish, ca. 1844

CHARLES BAUDELAIRE (1821–1867)

Photograph by Félix Nadar, 1855

L'ALBATROS

Souvent, pour s'amuser, les hommes d'équipage
Prennent des albatros, vastes oiseaux des mers,
Qui suivent, indolents compagnons de voyage,
Le navire glissant sur les gouffres amers.

A peine les ont-ils déposés sur les planches
Que ces rois de l'azur, maladroits et honteux,
Laissent piteusement leurs grandes ailes blanches
Comme des avirons traîner à côté d'eux.

Ce voyageur ailé, comme il est gauche et veule !
Lui, naguère si beau, qu'il est comique et laid !
L'un agace son bec avec un brûle-gueule,
L'autre mime en boitant l'infirme qui volait !

Le poète est semblable au prince des nuées,
Qui hante la tempête et se rit de l'archer ;
Exilé sur le sol au milieu des huées,
Ses ailes de géant l'empêchent de marcher.

THE ALBATROSS

Often, to pass the time, seafarers will ensnare
An albatross, that giant bird whose great wings sweep
In carefree indolence a passage through the air,
Behind the ship that glides upon the bitter deep.

No sooner have they been set down upon the boards
Than these kings of the blue, now clumsy and forlorn,
Let their enormous wings, like useless trailing oars,
Pathetically drag beside their graceless form.

This once proud voyager has now become a freak!
Erstwhile so elegant, now mocked and travestied!
One of them, with a pipe, callously prods its beak,
Another stoops to ape the limping invalid!

The poet is akin to this prince of the clouds
Who scorns the bowman's shaft and braves the stormy day;
In exile on the earth amid the baying crowds,
He cannot walk: his giant's wings get in the way.

CORRESPONDANCES

La Nature est un temple où de vivants piliers
Laissent parfois sortir de confuses paroles ;
L'homme y passe à travers des forêts de symboles
Qui l'observent avec des regards familiers.

Comme de longs échos qui de loin se confondent
Dans une ténébreuse et profonde unité,
Vaste comme la nuit et comme la clarté,
Les parfums, les couleurs et les sons se répondent.

Il est des parfums frais comme des chairs d'enfants,
Doux comme les hautbois, verts comme les prairies,
— Et d'autres, corrompus, riches et triomphants,

Ayant l'expansion des choses infinies,
Comme l'ambre, le musc, le benjoin et l'encens,
Qui chantent les transports de l'esprit et des sens.

CORRESPONDENCES

Nature is a temple, where living colonnades
May sometimes utter words in which confusion lies;
Man wanders through its forests, where symbolic eyes
Observe him knowingly with their familiar gaze.

Like long, resounding echoes from the far beyond
That merge into a deep, tenebrous unity,
Immense as night and vast as daylight's clarity,
All colours, fragrances and accents correspond.

Some perfumes are as pure and cool as infants' flesh,
Soft as the oboe's sound, as meadows green and fresh,
— And others, rich, corrupt, triumphant, dissolute,

With the expansive range of all things infinite,
Like amber resin, musk, benzoin, and frankincense,
That sing euphoric hymns to spirit, mind, and sense.

RECUEILLEMENT

Sois sage, ô ma Douleur, et tiens-toi plus tranquille.
Tu réclamais le Soir ; il descend ; le voici :
Une atmosphère obscure enveloppe la ville,
Aux uns portant la paix, aux autres le souci.

Pendant que des mortels la multitude vile,
Sous le fouet du Plaisir, ce bourreau sans merci,
Va cueillir des remords dans la fête servile,
Ma Douleur, donne-moi la main ; viens par ici,

Loin d'eux. Vois se pencher les défuntes Années,
Sur les balcons du ciel, en robes surannées ;
Surgir du fond des eaux le Regret souriant ;

Le Soleil moribond s'endormir sous une arche,
Et, comme un long linceul traînant à l'Orient,
Entends, ma chère, entends la douce Nuit qui marche.

REFLECTION

Be gentle, O my Sorrow; come now, settle down.
You longed for Eventide; her shadows fill the air;
A shroud of darkness now descends upon the town,
To some affording peace, to others only care.

And while of mortal man the wanton multitude,
Beneath the cruel scourge of Pleasure's tyranny,
Goes garnering remorse in servile turpitude,
My Sorrow, take my hand, and come away with me,

Far from them. See the bygone Years their vigil keep,
On heaven's balconies, in antiquated dress,
As simpering Regret emerges from the deep;

The Sun beneath an arch yields its expiring light,
And, like an endless shroud unwinding to the East,
Hear now, my dear, the gentle footsteps of the Night.

LE BALCON

Mère des souvenirs, maîtresse des maîtresses,
Ô toi, tous mes plaisirs ! ô toi, tous mes devoirs !
Tu te rappelleras la beauté des caresses,
La douceur du foyer et le charme des soirs,
Mère des souvenirs, maîtresse des maîtresses !

Les soirs illuminés par l'ardeur du charbon,
Et les soirs au balcon, voilés de vapeurs roses.
Que ton sein m'était doux ! que ton cœur m'était bon !
Nous avons dit souvent d'impérissables choses
Les soirs illuminés par l'ardeur du charbon.

Que les soleils sont beaux dans les chaudes soirées !
Que l'espace est profond ! que le cœur est puissant !
En me penchant vers toi, reine des adorées,
Je croyais respirer le parfum de ton sang.
Que les soleils sont beaux dans les chaudes soirées !

La nuit s'épaississait ainsi qu'une cloison,
Et mes yeux dans le noir devinaient tes prunelles,
Et je buvais ton souffle, ô douceur ! ô poison !
Et tes pieds s'endormaient dans mes mains fraternelles.
La nuit s'épaississait ainsi qu'une cloison.

Je sais l'art d'évoquer les minutes heureuses,
Et revis mon passé blotti dans tes genoux.
Car à quoi bon chercher tes beautés langoureuses
Ailleurs qu'en ton cher corps et qu'en ton cœur si doux ?
Je sais l'art d'évoquer les minutes heureuses !

Ces serments, ces parfums, ces baisers infinis,
Renaîtront-ils d'un gouffre interdit à nos sondes,
Comme montent au ciel les soleils rajeunis
Après s'être lavés au fond des mers profondes ?
— Ô serments ! ô parfums ! ô baisers infinis !

THE BALCONY

Mother of memories, mistress of mistresses,
O you my every bliss, O you my every duty,
You will recall the joy of our fervent caresses,
The comfort of the hearth, the evening's tranquil beauty,
Mother of memories, mistress of mistresses!

The evenings by the fire, lit by the burning coal,
And on the balcony, veiled in a rosy hue,
The softness of your breast, the sweetness of your soul!
We said so many things that are forever true,
The evenings by the fire, lit by the burning coal!

How beautiful the sunlight on a summer's night!
How deep the vault of heaven! How strong the beating heart!
Holding you close to me, O queen of my delight,
It seemed your very blood did its sweet scent impart.
How beautiful the sunlight on a summer's night!

The wall of darkness thickened, shutting out the light,
And in the gloom my eyes sought your eyes longingly,
And I imbibed your breath, O poisonous delight!
And in my loving hands your feet slept peacefully.
The wall of darkness thickened, shutting out the light.

The recollection of sweet moments is an art
That lets me live again those hours of happiness.
Why should I seek elsewhere than in your loving heart,
And in your gracious form, the joys of languidness?
The recollection of sweet moments is an art!

Those vows, those fragrant scents, those kisses without end,
Can they be born again from gulfs we cannot sound,
Just as the endless seas back to the heavens send
Rejuvenated suns that from their depths rebound?
— O vows! O fragrant scents! O kisses without end!

L'INVITATION AU VOYAGE

Mon enfant, ma sœur,
Songe à la douceur
D'aller là-bas vivre ensemble !
Aimer à loisir,
Aimer et mourir
Au pays qui te ressemble !
Les soleils mouillés
De ces ciels brouillés
Pour mon esprit ont les charmes
Si mystérieux
De tes traîtres yeux,
Brillant à travers leurs larmes.

Là, tout n'est qu'ordre et beauté,
Luxe, calme et volupté.

Des meubles luisants,
Polis par les ans,
Décoreraient notre chambre ;
Les plus rares fleurs
Mêlant leurs odeurs
Aux vagues senteurs de l'ambre,
Les riches plafonds,
Les miroirs profonds,
La splendeur orientale,
Tout y parlerait
À l'âme en secret
Sa douce langue natale.

Là, tout n'est qu'ordre et beauté,
Luxe, calme et volupté.

INVITATION TO A JOURNEY

My sister, my heart,
How sweet to depart
To that faraway haven with you!
To languidly lie,
To love and to die
In a land that resembles you!
The damp suns that rise
In those nebulous skies
Seem to mirror the charm that appears
In the mystic disguise
Of your treacherous eyes,
Glistening through their tears.

There, all is order and beauty,
Luxury, calm and ecstasy.

Furnishings fine,
Embellished by time,
Would decorate our room;
And flowers most rare
Their fragrance would share
With amber's heady perfume;
Ceilings ornate,
And walls with the weight
Of Orient's splendour hung;
All things there would speak
In the secret mystique
Of their gentle native tongue.

There, all is order and beauty,
Luxury, calm, and ecstasy.

L'INVITATION AU VOYAGE

Vois sur ces canaux
Dormir ces vaisseaux
Dont l'humeur est vagabonde ;
C'est pour assouvir
Ton moindre désir
Qu'ils viennent du bout du monde.
— Les soleils couchants
Revêtent les champs,
Les canaux, la ville entière,
D'hyacinthe et d'or ;
Le monde s'endort
Dans une chaude lumière.

Là, tout n'est qu'ordre et beauté,
Luxe, calme et volupté.

INVITATION TO A JOURNEY

See the vessels that brave
The wind and the wave
Rocking gently in their berth;
It is to inspire
Your every desire
That they come from the ends of the earth.
— The sun goes down,
Setting the town,
The meadows and rivers alight
With jacinth and gold;
Our dreams unfold
In a gently warming light.

There, all is order and beauty,
Luxury, calm and ecstasy.

Henri Matisse

À UNE PASSANTE

La rue assourdissante autour de moi hurlait.
Longue, mince, en grand deuil, douleur majestueuse,
Une femme passa, d'une main fastueuse
Soulevant, balançant le feston et l'ourlet ;

Agile et noble, avec sa jambe de statue.
Moi, je buvais, crispé comme un extravagant,
Dans son œil, ciel livide où germe l'ouragan,
La douceur qui fascine et le plaisir qui tue.

Un éclair... puis la nuit ! — Fugitive beauté
Dont le regard m'a fait soudainement renaître,
Ne te verrai-je plus que dans l'éternité ?

Ailleurs, bien loin d'ici ! trop tard ! *jamais* peut-être !
Car j'ignore où tu fuis, tu ne sais où je vais,
Ô toi que j'eusse aimée, ô toi qui le savais !

TO A PASSER-BY

About me roared the noise and clamour of the town.
A widow, new-bereaved, tall, slender, stately, grand,
Passed by, and with a florid gesture of her hand,
Lifted and flounced the scalloped border of her gown.

Enchanted by her grace, her perfect symmetry,
Delirious, I drank, enraptured yet forlorn,
From her eyes, livid skies where hurricanes are born,
The sweetness that enthrals, the lethal ecstasy.

A lightning flash... then night! — O fugitive beauty
Whose transitory glance kindled new life in me,
Shall I see you again but in eternity?

Elsewhere, so far from here! Too late! *Never*, maybe?
For I know not your fate, nor you my destiny,
You whom I might have loved, you knew it, fleetingly!

Henri Matisse

RÊVE PARISIEN
À Constantin Guys

I

De ce terrible paysage,
Tel que jamais mortel n'en vit,
Ce matin encore l'image,
Vague et lointaine, me ravit.

Le sommeil est plein de miracles !
Par un caprice singulier,
J'avais banni de ces spectacles
Le végétal irrégulier,

Et, peintre fier de mon génie,
Je savourais dans mon tableau
L'enivrante monotonie
Du métal, du marbre et de l'eau.

Babel d'escaliers et d'arcades,
C'était un palais infini,
Plein de bassins et de cascades
Tombant dans l'or mat ou bruni ;

Et des cataractes pesantes,
Comme des rideaux de cristal,
Se suspendaient, éblouissantes,
A des murailles de métal.

Non d'arbres, mais de colonnades
Les étangs dormants s'entouraient,
Où de gigantesques naïades,
Comme des femmes, se miraient.

Des nappes d'eau s'épanchaient, bleues,
Entre des quais roses et verts,
Pendant des millions de lieues,
Vers les confins de l'univers ;

C'étaient des pierres inouïes
Et des flots magiques ; c'étaient

A PARISIAN DREAM
To Constantin Guys

I

Of that most awe-inspiring scene,
Such as mere mortals never see,
That lay before me in a dream,
The image still enraptures me.

Sleep is a miracle divine!
And, by a singular caprice,
I had excluded any sign
Of vegetation from the piece;

And, proud of my fine artistry,
I savoured in this rare tableau
The breathtaking monotony
Of metal, stone, and water-flow.

Babel of stairways and arcades
And endless palaces unrolled,
With limpid pools and great cascades
Falling on matte or burnished gold;

And even greater waterfalls,
Like crystal curtains hanging there,
Cascaded down metallic walls
As if suspended in the air.

The dormant pools, instead of trees
Were circumscribed by colonnades,
Where giant naiads took their ease,
Admiring their reflected gaze.

Lakes of blue water outward flowed
Between the rose and emerald quays,
Like an endless aquatic road,
To the earth's furthest boundaries;

Magical waves, embellished by
Exquisite gemstones that adorned

RÊVE PARISIEN

D'immenses glaces éblouies
Par tout ce qu'elles reflétaient !

Insouciants et taciturnes,
Des Ganges, dans le firmament,
Versaient le trésor de leurs urnes
Dans des gouffres de diamant.

Architecte de mes féeries,
Je faisais, à ma volonté,
Sous un tunnel de pierreries
Passer un océan dompté ;

Et tout, même la couleur noire,
Semblait fourbi, clair, irisé ;
Le liquide enchâssait sa gloire
Dans le rayon cristallisé.

Nul astre d'ailleurs, nuls vestiges
De soleil, même au bas du ciel,
Pour illuminer ces prodiges,
Qui brillaient d'un feu personnel !

Et sur ces mouvantes merveilles
Planait (terrible nouveauté !
Tout pour l'œil, rien pour les oreilles !)
Un silence d'éternité.

II

En rouvrant mes yeux pleins de flamme
J'ai vu l'horreur de mon taudis,
Et senti, rentrant dans mon âme,
La pointe des soucis maudits ;

La pendule aux accents funèbres
Sonnait brutalement midi,
Et le ciel versait des ténèbres
Sur ce triste monde engourdi.

A PARISIAN DREAM

Enormous mirrors, dazzled by
The radiance of reflected forms.

Insouciant and taciturn,
Ganges flowed in the firmament,
Pouring the treasures from its urn
Into great gulfs of diamond.

Architect of my fantasy,
I made, out of a quiet rill,
To flow within an artery
An ocean I could tame at will;

And all the colours, even black,
Seemed iridescent, burnished bright;
The liquid gave its splendour back
In crystal rays of purest light.

No moon, no stars, nor any sign
Of sunlight to give luminance
To this prodigious scene of mine
That shone with its own radiance.

And on this wondrous vision here
There hovered (awful novelty!
All for the eye, naught for the ear!)
A silence of eternity.

II

I opened my bewildered eyes
And saw again the wretched hole
Wherein I dwelt, and felt arise
The pangs of anguish in my soul;

The melancholy clock struck noon
In accents brutal and perverse,
And from the sky a dreadful gloom
Pervaded the dull universe.

LE VOYAGE
À Maxime Du Camp

I

Pour l'enfant, amoureux de cartes et d'estampes,
L'univers est égal à son vaste appétit.
Ah! que le monde est grand à la clarté des lampes !
Aux yeux du souvenir que le monde est petit !

Un matin nous partons, le cerveau plein de flamme,
Le cœur gros de rancune et de désirs amers,
Et nous allons, suivant le rythme de la lame,
Berçant notre infini sur le fini des mers :

Les uns, joyeux de fuir une patrie infâme ;
D'autres, l'horreur de leurs berceaux, et quelques-uns,
Astrologues noyés dans les yeux d'une femme,
La Circé tyrannique aux dangereux parfums.

Pour n'être pas changés en bêtes, ils s'enivrent
D'espace et de lumière et de cieux embrasés ;
La glace qui les mord, les soleils qui les cuivrent
Effacent lentement la marque des baisers.

Mais les vrais voyageurs sont ceux-là seuls qui partent
Pour partir ; cœurs légers, semblables aux ballons,
De leur fatalité jamais ils ne s'écartent,
Et, sans savoir pourquoi, disent toujours : « Allons! »

Ceux-là dont les désirs ont la forme des nues,
Et qui rêvent, ainsi qu'un conscrit le canon,
De vastes voluptés, changeantes, inconnues,
Et dont l'esprit humain n'a jamais su le nom !

II

Nous imitons, horreur ! la toupie et la boule
Dans leur valse et leurs bonds ; même dans nos sommeils
La Curiosité nous tourmente et nous roule,
Comme un Ange cruel qui fouette des soleils.

THE VOYAGE
To Maxime Du Camp

I

For children who delight in maps and colour plates,
The world is equal only to their appetite.
Bright lights can make it seem such an enormous place!
And yet how small it is, considered with hindsight!

One morning we depart, our ardent minds afire,
Carried on waves that rise and fall rhythmically,
Our hearts beset by rancour and bitter desire,
Cradling infinite thoughts upon a finite sea:

Some of us, glad to flee a country we despise,
Others, the horror of their birthplace, others still,
Astrologers immersed in a strange woman's eyes,
Subjected to the tyranny of perfumed Circe's will.

In order not to be transmuted into swine,
They drink their fill of light from lambent realms of space;
The biting winds, the searing suns that bronze their skin,
Slowly erase the marks left by her vile embrace.

But the true voyagers are those who put to sea
Simply for travel's sake; they press on, hearts aglow;
They never leave the path of their true destiny,
And though they know not why, they always say: Let's go!

Those whose intense desires resemble cumulus,
Who, like a new recruit who dreams about the gun,
Foresee unending pleasures, vast, voluptuous,
The names of which remain unknown to anyone!

II

We imitate, O horror! balls and spinning tops
That, even while we sleep, gyrate and bounce and run,
And Curiosity, cruel Angel, never stops
Tormenting us, like suns that she has whipped and spun.

LE VOYAGE

Singulière fortune, où le but se déplace
Et, n'étant nulle part, peut être n'importe où !
Où l'Homme, dont jamais l'espérance n'est lasse,
Pour trouver le repos court toujours comme un fou !

Notre âme est un trois-mâts cherchant son Icarie ;
Une voix retentit sur le pont: « Ouvre l'œil ! »
Une voix de la hune, ardente et folle, crie :
« Amour... gloire... bonheur! » Enfer ! c'est un écueil

Chaque îlot signalé par l'homme de vigie
Est un Eldorado promis par le Destin;
L'Imagination qui dresse son orgie
Ne trouve qu'un récif aux clartés du matin.

Ô le pauvre amoureux des pays chimériques !
Faut-il le mettre aux fers, le jeter à la mer,
Ce matelot ivrogne, inventeur d'Amériques
Dont le mirage rend le gouffre plus amer ?

Tel le vieux vagabond, piétinant dans la boue,
Rêve, le nez en l'air, de brillants paradis ;
Son œil ensorcelé découvre une Capoue
Partout où la chandelle illumine un taudis.

III

Étonnants voyageurs ! quelles nobles histoires
Nous lisons dans vos yeux profonds comme les mers !
Montrez-nous les écrins de vos riches mémoires,
Ces bijoux merveilleux, faits d'astres et d'éthers.

Nous voulons voyager sans vapeur et sans voile !
Faites, pour égayer l'ennui de nos prisons,
Passer sur nos esprits, tendus comme une toile,
Vos souvenirs avec leurs cadres d'horizons.

THE VOYAGE

Strange destiny whose goal is always on the move,
And being nowhere, can be anywhere, who knows?
Where Man, whose steadfast hope no obstacle can move,
Continues his eternal quest to find repose!

Our soul is like a ship that seeks Icaria;
"Look there!" someone on deck shouts out in disbelief.
While from the mast come cries of great euphoria:
"O joy and happiness!" — Damnation! It's a reef!

Each tiny island that the lookout boy might see
Is taken to be Eldorado, our last dock;
Imagination, spreading out its panoply,
In the cold light of day finds nothing but a rock.

O that poor lover of exotic chimeras!
Should we clap him in irons and cast him to the sea,
That drunken sailor who sees new Americas
Whose mirage makes the oceans flow more bitterly?

So too the aged vagrant, trudging through the mud,
Dreaming, nose in the air, of heavens bathed in light;
His ever-spellbound eye sees a new Capua
In every humble dwelling lit by candlelight.

III

Amazing voyagers! What noble histories
We read in the unfathomed oceans of your eyes!
Open for us the caskets of your memories,
Those wondrous treasures that are made from stars and skies.

We too, with neither steam nor sail, would cross the seas!
To lighten our ennui, where every day's the same,
Paint on the canvas of our hearts your memories
Of all the wonders that the vast horizons frame.

LE VOYAGE

Dites, qu'avez-vous vu ?
IV
« Nous avons vu des astres
Et des flots; nous avons vu des sables aussi ;
Et, malgré bien des chocs et d'imprévus désastres,
Nous nous sommes souvent ennuyés, comme ici.

La gloire du soleil sur la mer violette,
La gloire des cités dans le soleil couchant,
Allumaient dans nos cœurs une ardeur inquiète
De plonger dans un ciel au reflet alléchant.

Les plus riches cités, les plus grands paysages
Jamais ne contenaient l'attrait mystérieux
De ceux que le hasard fait avec les nuages,
Et toujours le désir nous rendait soucieux !

— La jouissance ajoute au désir de la force.
Désir, vieil arbre à qui le plaisir sert d'engrais,
Cependant que grossit et durcit ton écorce,
Tes branches veulent voir le soleil de plus près !

Grandiras-tu toujours, grand arbre plus vivace
Que le cyprès ? — Pourtant nous avons, avec soin,
Cueilli quelques croquis pour votre album vorace,
Frères qui trouvez beau tout ce qui vient de loin !

— Nous avons salué des idoles à trompe,
Des trônes constellés de joyaux lumineux ;
Des palais ouvragés dont la féerique pompe
Serait pour vos banquiers un rêve ruineux ;

Des costumes qui sont pour les yeux une ivresse ;
Des femmes dont les dents et les ongles sont teints,
Et des jongleurs savants que le serpent caresse. »

THE VOYAGE

Tell us, what have you seen?
IV
"We have seen many stars
And many waves; we have seen many beaches too;
And despite many blows, of which we bear the scars,
We often felt the weight of boredom, just like you.

The glory of the sun's rays on the violet sea,
The glory of the cities that in the sunset rise,
Ignited in our hearts a strange anxiety
To plunge into the depths of those alluring skies.

Great vistas and great cities, rich in history,
Could never hold for us the mystical allure
Of scenes formed by the clouds, so full of mystery.
And longing always left us anxious and unsure!

— Enjoyment bolsters up and strengthens our desire.
Desire, old tree for whom delight is your manure,
Your bark grows thick and hard, and your branches grow higher,
Striving to reach the sky, drawn by the sun's allure.

Will you grow ever taller, great tree more robust
Than even the cypress? — But from our wanderings
We've saved some sketches for your album, you who must
Indulge your avid yearnings for exotic things!

We've bowed to graven images and effigies;
Fine thrones inset with gems of quality supreme;
Imposing palaces whose fabled luxuries
Would be for any banker a ruinous dream;

Costumes that are inebriation for the eyes;
Women with teeth and nails tinted with subtle stains,
And snake charmers whose skills astonish and surprise."

LE VOYAGE

V
Et puis, et puis encore ?
VI
« O cerveaux enfantins !

Pour ne pas oublier la chose capitale,
Nous avons vu partout, et sans l'avoir cherché,
Du haut jusques en bas de l'échelle fatale,
Le spectacle ennuyeux de l'immortel péché :

La femme, esclave vile, orgueilleuse et stupide,
Sans rire s'adorant et s'aimant sans dégoût ;
L'homme, tyran goulu, paillard, dur et cupide,
Esclave de l'esclave et ruisseau dans l'égout ;

Le bourreau qui jouit, le martyr qui sanglote ;
La fête qu'assaisonne et parfume le sang ;
Le poison du pouvoir énervant le despote,
Et le peuple amoureux du fouet abrutissant ;

Plusieurs religions semblables à la nôtre,
Toutes escaladant le ciel ; la Sainteté,
Comme en un lit de plume un délicat se vautre,
Dans les clous et le crin cherchant la volupté ;

L'Humanité bavarde, ivre de son génie,
Et, folle maintenant comme elle était jadis,
Criant à Dieu, dans sa furibonde agonie :
O mon semblable, ô mon maître, je te maudis !

Et les moins sots, hardis amants de la Démence,
Fuyant le grand troupeau parqué par le Destin,
Et se réfugiant dans l'opium immense !
— Tel est du globe entier l'éternel bulletin. »

THE VOYAGE

V
And then, and then what else?
VI
"O simple childlike brains!

We never should forget the most important thing:
Across the entire spectrum of humanity,
We witnessed, without seeking, in our wandering,
The tedious round of sin and immorality:

Woman, base slave, self-loving and contemptuous,
Yet unaware that she's so stupid and so vain;
And man, obsessed by greed, wanton, libidinous,
Slave of the slave and gutter flowing in the drain;

The torturer's delight, the martyr's agony;
The feast seasoned with blood to feed the despot's urge;
The lust for power and the curse of tyranny,
The crowd enamoured of the brutalising scourge;

Many religions that are not unlike our own,
All aiming for the sky; and Saintly Piety,
Like a voluptuary upon a bed of down,
In nails and sackcloth seeking joy and ecstasy;

Drunk on its genius, prattling Humanity,
That's just as crazy now as it's been from the first,
Shouting to God, in its unbridled agony:
O Master, my own likeness, may you now be cursed!

And those less stupid, brave friends of Insanity,
Fleeing the servile flock that Fate has herded in,
And seeking refuge in opium's sanctuary!
— Such is the entire globe's eternal bulletin."

LE VOYAGE

VII

Amer savoir, celui qu'on tire du voyage !
Le monde, monotone et petit, aujourd'hui,
Hier, demain, toujours, nous fait voir notre image :
Une oasis d'horreur dans un désert d'ennui !

Faut-il partir ? Rester ? Si tu peux rester, reste ;
Pars, s'il le faut. L'un court, et l'autre se tapit
Pour tromper l'ennemi vigilant et funeste,
Le Temps ! Il est, hélas ! des coureurs sans répit,

Comme le Juif errant et comme les apôtres,
A qui rien ne suffit, ni wagon, ni vaisseau,
Pour fuir ce rétiaire infâme ; il en est d'autres
Qui savent le tuer sans quitter leur berceau.

Lorsque enfin il mettra le pied sur notre échine,
Nous pourrons espérer et crier : En avant !
De même qu'autrefois nous partions pour la Chine,
Les yeux fixés au large et les cheveux au vent,

Nous nous embarquerons sur la mer des Ténèbres
Avec le cœur joyeux d'un jeune passager.
Entendez-vous ces voix, charmantes et funèbres,
Qui chantent : « Par ici ! vous qui voulez manger

Le Lotus parfumé: c'est ici qu'on vendange
Les fruits miraculeux dont votre cœur a faim ;
Venez vous enivrer de la douceur étrange
De cette après-midi qui n'a jamais de fin. »

A l'accent familier nous devinons le spectre ;
Nos Pylades là-bas tendent leurs bras vers nous.
« Pour rafraîchir ton cœur nage vers ton Électre ! »
Dit celle dont jadis nous baisions les genoux.

THE VOYAGE

VII

Such bitter knowledge that we all draw from our voyage!
The world, monotonous and petty, lets us see,
Today, yesterday and tomorrow, our own image:
An oasis of horror in a desert of ennui!

Should we depart? or stay? If you can't stay, then go;
Stay if you can. One runs, another secretly
Remains to thwart harsh Time, that unrelenting foe!
There are, alas! those who are running constantly,

Like the apostles or the lonely wandering Jew,
To whom nothing avails, neither carriage nor ship,
To flee this vicious combatant; there are a few
Who know how to dispatch him without leaving their crib.

When finally he catches up with us, at least
We shall still foster hope, and shout aloud: Let's go!
Just as in former times we set off for the East,
Eyes fixed on the horizon, and with cheeks aglow

We shall embark upon the Sea of Darkness, where
We'll sail, like a young passenger, in joyful haste.
Do you hear those beguiling, deathlike voices there,
That sing: "This way please, those of you who wish to taste

The perfumed Lotus! This is where we gather in
The wondrous fruits whose flavour every joy transcends.
Come and taste their delights, forever savouring
The magic of an afternoon that never ends!"

In those familiar tones we recognise the spectre;
Our friends, like Pylades, stretch out their arms to us.
"To replenish your heart, swim out to your Electra!"
Says she whose knees in former times we used to kiss.

LE VOYAGE

VIII

Ô Mort, vieux capitaine, il est temps ! levons l'ancre !
Ce pays nous ennuie, ô Mort ! Appareillons !
Si le ciel et la mer sont noirs comme de l'encre,
Nos cœurs que tu connais sont remplis de rayons !

Verse-nous ton poison pour qu'il nous réconforte !
Nous voulons, tant ce feu nous brûle le cerveau,
Plonger au fond du gouffre, Enfer ou Ciel, qu'importe ?
Au fond de l'Inconnu pour trouver du *nouveau* !

THE VOYAGE

VIII

O Death, old captain, let's cast off! The time has come!
This country holds no joy for us. Come! Let's depart!
Although both sea and sky are bathed in inky gloom,
You know that your bright flame still burns in every heart!

Pour us your poisoned draught, and let its comfort dwell
Within us; let your ardent fire our hearts imbue;
We'll plunge into the gulf, what matter Heaven or Hell?
Of the immense Unknown, in search of something *new*!

Vaslav Nijinsky as the Faun in the ballet 'L'après-midi d'un faune', by the Ballet Russe, Paris, 1912. The ballet was choreographed by Nijinsky himself.

A cartoon by Daniel de Losques for *Le Figaro*, 1912

STÉPHANE MALLARMÉ (1842 – 1898)

From a painting by Édouard Manet

L'APRÈS-MIDI D'UN FAUNE

Édouard Manet

Le Faune

Ces nymphes, je les veux perpétuer.
                                    Si clair,
Leur incarnat léger, qu'il voltige dans l'air
Assoupi de sommeils touffus.
                                          Aimai-je un rêve ?
Mon doute, amas de nuit ancienne, s'achève
En maint rameau subtil, qui, demeuré les vrais
Bois même, prouve, hélas ! que bien seul je m'offrais
Pour triomphe la faute idéale de roses —
Réfléchissons...
                    ou si les femmes dont tu gloses
Figurent un souhait de tes sens fabuleux !
Faune, l'illusion s'échappe des yeux bleus
Et froids, comme une source en pleurs, de la plus chaste :
Mais, l'autre tout soupirs, dis-tu qu'elle contraste
Comme brise du jour chaude dans ta toison ?
Que non! par l'immobile et lasse pâmoison
Suffoquant de chaleurs le matin frais s'il lutte,
Ne murmure point d'eau que ne verse ma flute
Au bosquet arrosé d'accords ; et le seul vent
Hors des deux tuyaux prompt à s'exhaler avant

THE AFTERNOON OF A FAUN

Édouard Manet

The Faun

These nymphs I would they were perpetual.
                                    So clear,
Their rose-hued slenderness, it flutters in the air
Somnolent in thick tufts of sleep.
                            Loved I a dream?
My doubt, garner of erstwhile night, would surely seem
To end in many a subtle branch that, staying true
To their same wood must prove, alas! that I alone
As triumph gave myself the false idealised rose —
Let's see…
            What if the women you so idolise
Are merely figments of your fabulous desires!
Faun, the illusion flows from eyes so blue and cold,
As from a weeping spring, of her who is most chaste:
The other, full of sighs, you say that she contrasts
Like a warm daytime breeze that plays upon your fleece?
But no! If the cool morn combats the stifling heat
Against the motionless and swooning weariness,
No water murmurs save that which flows from my flute
That floods the grove with melodies; alone the wind
From those twin pipes exhales so readily before

L'APRÈS-MIDI D'UN FAUNE

Qu'il disperse le son dans une pluie aride,
C'est, à l'horizon pas remué d'une ride
Le visible et serein souffle artificiel
De l'inspiration, qui regagne le ciel.

O bords siciliens d'un calme marécage
Qu'à l'envi de soleils ma vanité saccage
Tacite sous les fleurs d'étincelles, CONTEZ
« Que je coupais ici les creux roseaux domptés
Par le talent; quand, sur l'or glauque de lointaines
Verdures dédiant leur vigne à des fontaines,
Ondoie une blancheur animale au repos :
Et qu'au prélude lent où naissent les pipeaux
Ce vol de cygnes, non! de naïades se sauve
Ou plonge...
               Inerte, tout brûle dans l'heure fauve
Sans marquer par quel art ensemble détala
Trop d'hymen souhaité de qui cherche le la :
Alors m'éveillerai-je à la ferveur première,
Droit et seul, sous un flot antique de lumière,
Lys! et l'un de vous tous pour l'ingénuité.

Autre que ce doux rien par leur lèvre ébruité,
Le baiser, qui tout bas des perfides assure,
Mon sein, vierge de preuve, atteste une morsure
Mystérieuse, due à quelque auguste dent ;
Mais, bast! arcane tel élut pour confident
Le jonc vaste et jumeau dont sous l'azur on joue :
Qui, détournant à soi le trouble de la joue,
Rêve, dans un solo long, que nous amusions
La beauté d'alentour par des confusions
Fausses entre elle-même et notre chant crédule ;
Et de faire aussi haut que l'amour se module
Évanouir du songe ordinaire de dos
Ou de flanc pur suivis avec mes regards clos,

THE AFTERNOON OF A FAUN

Dispersing all its sounds in arid drops of rain,
It is, on the horizon where no ripple moves
The artificial breath, visible and serene,
Of inspiration that regains the firmament.

O calm Sicilian shores of marsh serene and still
That vying with the sun my vanity despoils
Tacit beneath the scintillating flowers, TELL
"That I was cutting here the hollow reeds I tamed
By talent; when, in the vague haze the blue-green gold
Of distant verdant hills to founts offering their vines,
There undulates the white of animals at rest:
And in the lazy prelude where the reeds are born
This flock of swans, but no! of naiads taking flight
Or diving...
           Motionless, all burns this tawny hour
With no trace of the art by which together fled
Too much hymen desired by him who seeks the la:
Then shall I wake unto the quintessential fervour,
Upright, alone, beneath an ancient stream of light,
Lily! at one with you in pure naïveté.

Other than this sweet nothing escaping from their lips,
The kiss, that quietly assures perfidity,
My breast, virgin of proof, bears witness to a bite,
Mysterious, the fruit of some exalted tooth;
But cease! for the arcane chose as it's confidant
The great twin reed we play beneath the azure blue:
Which, turning back the troubled cheek unto itself,
Dreams, in a solo long, that we did entertain
The beauty all around with false bewilderment
Between itself and this our most spontaneous song;
And so to cause, as high as love itself can sing,
To fade from mundane dream of pure unsullied loin
Or flank that I pursue with my clandestine gaze,

L'APRÈS-MIDI D'UN FAUNE

Une sonore, vaine et monotone ligne.

Tâche donc, instrument des fuites, ô maligne
Syrinx, de refleurir aux lacs où tu m'attends !
Moi, de ma rumeur fier, je vais parler longtemps
Des déesses ; et par d'idolâtres peintures
À leur ombre enlever encore des ceintures :
Ainsi, quand des raisins j'ai sucé la clarté,
Pour bannir un regret par ma feinte écarté,
Rieur, j'élève au ciel d'été la grappe vide
Et, soufflant dans ses peaux lumineuses, avide
D'ivresse, jusqu'au soir je regarde au travers.

O nymphes, regonflons des SOUVENIRS divers.
Mon oeil, trouant les joncs, dardait chaque encolure
Immortelle, qui noie en l'onde sa brûlure
Avec un cri de rage au ciel de la forêt ;
Et le splendide bain de cheveux disparaît
Dans les clartés et les frissons, ô pierreries !
J'accours; quand, à mes pieds, s'entrejoignent (meurtries
De la langueur goûtée à ce mal d'être deux)
Des dormeuses parmi leurs seuls bras hasardeux ;
Je les ravis, sans les désenlacer, et vole
À ce massif, haï par l'ombrage frivole,
De roses tarissant tout parfum au soleil,
Où notre ébat au jour consumé soit pareil.
Je t'adore, courroux des vierges, ô délice
Farouche du sacré fardeau nu qui se glisse
Pour fuir ma lèvre en feu buvant, comme un éclair
Tressaille ! la frayeur secrète de la chair :
Des pieds de l'inhumaine au cœur de la timide
Qui délaisse à la fois une innocence, humide
De larmes folles ou de moins tristes vapeurs.
« Mon crime, c'est d'avoir, gai de vaincre ces peurs
Traîtresses, divisé la touffe échevelée
De baisers que les dieux gardaient si bien mêlée :

THE AFTERNOON OF A FAUN

A cadence, sonorous, vain and monotonous.

Strive then, O instrument of flight, malign Syrinx,
To flower again beside the lakes where you await me!
I, of my fable proud, shall long hold forth with tales
Of goddesses, and in idolatrous displays
From shadows of their form more girdles yet remove:
And so, when I have sucked the nectar from the grapes,
To banish a regret dismissed by my pretence,
Laughing, I raise the empty stem to summer's sky
And, blowing into skins translucent in the light,
Desiring drunkenness, gaze through them until dark.

O nymphs, let's give new breath to diverse MEMORIES.
"My eye, piercing the reeds, spears each immortal nape,
That seeks to drown the burn in waters of the lake
With cries of rage ascending to the forest sky;
And the resplendent tide of hair then disappears
In shimm'ring, thrilling shafts of light, O precious stones!
I hasten there; when, at my feet entwined (and bruised
By languor tasted in this ill of being twain)
Lie sleeping nymphs, defenceless, in each other's arms;
I seize them, leaving them entangled, and make haste
To this massif, abhorred by the frivolous shade,
Of roses giving up their perfume to the sun,
Where our sweet sport may vie with the departing day.
I love you, wrath of virgins, O what wild delight
Of this nude sacred burden that now slips away
To flee my burning lips that sup, as lightening thrills!
The enigmatic terror that pervades the flesh:
From the inhuman's feet to the timid one's heart,
Abandoning an innocence that's now both moist
With frenzied weeping or less melancholy tears.
My crime is, keen to conquer these treacherous fears,
To gaily disentangle the dishevelled tuft
Of kisses that the gods had kept so well enmeshed:

L'APRÈS-MIDI D'UN FAUNE

Car, à peine j'allais cacher un rire ardent
Sous les replis heureux d'une seule (gardant
Par un doigt simple, afin que sa candeur de plume
Se teignît à l'émoi de sa sœur qui s'allume,
La petite, naïve et ne rougissant pas :)
Que de mes bras, défaits par de vagues trépas,
Cette proie, à jamais ingrate se délivre
Sans pitié du sanglot dont j'étais encore ivre.

Tant pis ! vers le bonheur d'autres m'entraîneront
Par leur tresse nouée aux cornes de mon front :
Tu sais, ma passion, que, pourpre et déjà mûre,
Chaque grenade éclate et d'abeilles murmure ;
Et notre sang, épris de qui le va saisir,
Coule pour tout l'essaim éternel du désir.
À l'heure où ce bois d'or et de cendres se teinte
Une fête s'exalte en la feuillée éteinte :
Etna ! c'est parmi toi visité de Vénus
Sur ta lave posant tes talons ingénus,
Quand tonne une somme triste ou s'épuise la flamme.
Je tiens la reine !
                    O sûr châtiment...
                                        Non, mais l'âme
De paroles vacante et ce corps alourdi
Tard succombent au fier silence de midi :
Sans plus il faut dormir en l'oubli du blasphème,
Sur le sable altéré gisant et comme j'aime
Ouvrir ma bouche à l'astre efficace des vins !

Couple, adieu ; je vais voir l'ombre que tu devins.

THE AFTERNOON OF A FAUN

For, scarce had I begun bold laughter to conceal
Beneath the winsome folds of one of them (keeping
Beneath one finger, that her fragile candour might
Be tainted by the thrill that's kindled in her sister,
The innocent, naive, unblushing little one)
Than from my arms, undone by vague ideas of death,
This prey, eternally ungrateful, now breaks free,
Scorning the sob which still intoxicated me.

Too bad! To happiness by others I'll be led,
Their tresses knotted tight to the horns of my brow:
You know, my passion that, deep red and fully ripe,
Each pomegranate bursts with sounds of humming bees;
And our blood, enamoured of all who would it seize,
Flows for the whole eternal swarm of our desire.
At the hour when this wood is clothed in gold and ash
A glorious feast erupts in the dark leafy bower:
Etna! It's on your slopes by Venus visited
As on your lava she sets down her artless heel,
When sad sleep rumbles on or the flame is snuffed out.
I hold the queen!
                O sure chastisement…
                                        No, the soul
Devoid of words and this my body now forlorn
Succumb belatedly to noon's proud quietude:
It is now time to sleep devoid of blasphemy,
Recumbent on the thirsting sand and as I love
Open my mouth unto the sovereign star of wine!

Couple, farewell; I go to see the shadow you became.

FEUILLET D'ALBUM

Tout à coup et comme par jeu
Mademoiselle qui voulûtes
Ouïr se révéler un peu
Le bois de mes diverses flûtes

Il me semble que cet essai
Tenté devant un paysage
A du bon quand je le cessai
Pour vous regarder au visage

Oui ce vain souffle que j'exclus
Jusqu'à la dernière limite
Selon mes quelques doigts perclus
Manque de moyens s'il imite

Votre très naturel et clair
Rire d'enfant qui charme l'air.

ALBUM LEAF

Suddenly as if in play
Mademoiselle you who would
desire to hear a tune today
from these my diverse flutes of wood

It seems to me that this assay
attempted in some rural place
should presently be cast away
to look more closely at your face

Yes this vain piping I suppressed
according to my fingers' limits
given their rheumatoid distress
is lacking in the means to mimic

Your very natural and clear
childlike laughter that charms the ear

Paul Verlaine and Jean Moréas in a gallery
Publicity lithograph for a Paris exhibition, 1894

PAUL VERLAINE (1844 – 1896)

Photograph by Alcide Allevy, 1883.

ART POÉTIQUE

De la musique avant toute chose,
Et pour cela préfère l'Impair
Plus vague et plus soluble dans l'air,
Sans rien en lui qui pèse ou qui pose.

Il faut aussi que tu n'ailles point
Choisir tes mots sans quelque méprise :
Rien de plus cher que la chanson grise
Où l'Indécis au Précis se joint.

C'est des beaux yeux derrière des voiles,
C'est le grand jour tremblant de midi,
C'est, par un ciel d'automne attiédi,
Le bleu fouillis des claires étoiles !

Car nous voulons la Nuance encor,
Pas la Couleur, rien que la nuance !
Oh ! la nuance seule fiance
Le rêve au rêve et la flûte au cor !

Fuis du plus loin la Pointe assassine,
L'Esprit cruel et le Rire impur,
Qui font pleurer les yeux de l'Azur,
Et tout cet ail de basse cuisine !

Prends l'éloquence et tords-lui son cou !
Tu feras bien, en train d'énergie,
De rendre un peu la Rime assagie.
Si l'on n'y veille, elle ira jusqu'où ?

Ô qui dira les torts de la Rime ?
Quel enfant sourd ou quel nègre fou
Nous a forgé ce bijou d'un sou
Qui sonne creux et faux sous la lime ?

THE ART OF POETRY

Above all let there music be,
Prefer uneven metre where
Vague sounds dissolve in the limpid air,
With nothing there that weighs heavily.

Take care with your phraseology,
Be neither too short nor overlong:
There's nothing more pleasing than the song
In which Doubt mingles with Certainty.

It's eyes that are veiled in mystery,
It's an ardent noon's pulsating light,
It is, in a cool autumn sky at night,
Stars casting their light more timidly.

For we prefer Nuance, subtlety,
Not Colour, just a nuance, a shade!
Only Nuance in dreams can wed
The flute and the horn in harmony.

Avoid harsh Scorn, and don't demean
With impure Laughter or callous Wit;
The eyes of the Azure will weep for it,
And all that garlic of bad cuisine!

Take eloquence and wring its neck!
You'd do better to use your energy
In choosing Rhyme more prudently.
Where will it lead if not kept in check?

O who will admit the ills of rhyme!
What deaf child or what simple fool
Has forged for us this worthless jewel
That sounds so false with its hollow chime?

ART POÉTIQUE

De la musique encore et toujours !
Que ton vers soit la chose envolée
Qu'on sent qui fuit d'une âme en allée
Vers d'autres cieux à d'autres amours.

Que ton vers soit la bonne aventure
Éparse au vent crispé du matin
Qui va fleurant la menthe et le thym…
Et tout le reste est littérature.

THE ART OF POETRY

Let music again and forever rise!
May your verse in its flight be something
That seems to flee from a soul that takes wing
Toward other loves in other skies.

May your verse be a great adventure
Scattered to the crisp morning breeze
Imbued with the fragrance of mint and thyme…
And all the rest is literature.

CHANSON D'AUTOMNE

Les sanglots longs
Des violons
De l'automne
Blessent mon cœur
D'une langueur
Monotone.

Tout suffocant
Et blême, quand
Sonne l'heure,
Je me souviens
Des jours anciens
Et je pleure ;

Et je m'en vais
Au vent mauvais
Qui m'emporte
Deçà, delà,
Pareil à la
Feuille morte.

AUTUMN SONG

The sighing
Of the fiddle's
Autumn song
Assails my heart
With languor
Dull and long.

Breathless and pale
When midnight's bell
Its vigil keeps,
I call to mind
Those former times
And my heart weeps;

And now I go
Where ill winds blow
Alone in grief,
Blown here and there
Just like
A fallen leaf.

MON RÊVE FAMILIER

Je fais souvent ce rêve étrange et pénétrant
D'une femme inconnue, et que j'aime, et qui m'aime,
Et qui n'est, chaque fois, ni tout à fait la même
Ni tout à fait une autre, et m'aime et me comprend.

Car elle me comprend, et mon cœur transparent
Pour elle seule, hélas ! cesse d'être un problème
Pour elle seule, et les moiteurs de mon front blême,
Elle seule les sait rafraîchir, en pleurant.

Est-elle brune, blonde ou rousse ? Je l'ignore.
Son nom ? Je me souviens qu'il est doux et sonore,
Comme ceux des aimés que la vie exila.

Son regard est pareil au regard des statues,
Et, pour sa voix, lointaine, et calme, et grave, elle a
L'inflexion des voix chères qui se sont tues.

MY FAMILIAR DREAM

I often have this strange and penetrating dream
About a woman, whom I love and who loves me,
And who, each time I dream, is never quite the same,
Nor is she yet another, and loves and understands me.

For she can understand me, and my heart that's clear
For her alone, alas, is not a problem now
For her, and the moist droplets of my pallid brow,
She only has the power to cool them with a tear.

Is her hair auburn, dark, or fair? - I do not know.
Her name? as I recall, its gentle accents flow
In names of those we loved, now banished from this life.

Her gaze is reminiscent of a statue's gaze,
And her voice, distant, calm and grave, reminds me of
The voices that I knew and loved in bygone days.

COLLOQUE SENTIMENTAL

Dans le vieux parc solitaire et glacé,
Deux formes ont tout à l'heure passé.

Leurs yeux sont morts et leurs lèvres sont molles,
Et l'on entend à peine leurs paroles.

Dans le vieux parc solitaire et glacé,
Deux spectres ont évoqué le passé.

– Te souvient-il de notre extase ancienne ?
– Pourquoi voulez-vous donc qu'il m'en souvienne ?

– Ton cœur bat-il toujours à mon seul nom ?
Toujours vois-tu mon âme en rêve ? – Non.

– Ah ! les beaux jours de bonheur indicible
Où nous joignions nos bouches ! – C'est possible.

– Qu'il était bleu, le ciel, et grand, l'espoir !
– L'espoir a fui, vaincu, vers le ciel noir.

Tels ils marchaient dans les avoines folles,
Et la nuit seule entendit leurs paroles.

A SENTIMENTAL COLLOQUY

Across the cold and lonely park
Two figures wander in the dark.

Their eyes are dead, their lips are grey,
They speak in whispers as they stray.

In sombre tones, with eyes downcast,
Two spectral forms evoke the past.

– Do you recall our ardent days?"
– No, why should I? the other says.

– And does not your blood faster flow
Just at the sound of my name? – No.

– And the sweet joy, ineffable,
When our lips met? – It's possible.

– The sky was blue, our hopes were high!
– Now to the dark sky hopes must fly.

And so they wander, out of sight,
Their words heard only by the night.

Il pleure dans mon cœur
Comme il pleut sur la ville ;
Quelle est cette langueur
Qui pénètre mon cœur ?

Ô bruit doux de la pluie
Par terre et sur les toits !
Pour un cœur qui s'ennuie,
Ô le chant de la pluie !

Il pleure sans raison
Dans ce cœur qui s'écœure.
Quoi ! nulle trahison ?...
Ce deuil est sans raison.

C'est bien la pire peine
De ne savoir pourquoi
Sans amour et sans haine
Mon cœur a tant de peine !

It weeps in my heart
As it rains on the town
What is this dull smart
That pierces my heart?

The soft sound of rain
On rooftop and street!
For a heart filled with pain,
O the song of the rain!

It weeps for no reason
In this heart that grows weary.
What? Is there no treason?...
This grief has no reason.

It is the worst pain
Not to know why
Without love or disdain
My heart feels such pain!

Drawing of Arthur Rimbaud by Paul Verlaine, 1872

ARTHUR RIMBAUD (1854 –1891)

Photograph by Étienne Carjat, 1872

LE DORMEUR DU VAL

C'est un trou de verdure où chante une rivière
Accrochant follement aux herbes des haillons
D'argent ; où le soleil, de la montagne fière,
Luit : c'est un petit val qui mousse de rayons.

Un soldat jeune, bouche ouverte, tête nue,
Et la nuque baignant dans le frais cresson bleu,
Dort ; il est étendu dans l'herbe, sous la nue,
Pâle dans son lit vert où la lumière pleut.

Les pieds dans les glaïeuls, il dort. Souriant comme
Sourirait un enfant malade, il fait un somme :
Nature, berce-le chaudement : il a froid.

Les parfums ne font pas frissonner sa narine ;
Il dort dans le soleil, la main sur sa poitrine
Tranquille. Il a deux trous rouges au côté droit.

THE SLEEPER IN THE VALLEY

It is a patch of green, beside a singing stream
That frantically clings to ragged silver rushes;
Where sunrays from the nearby mountain proudly gleam:
It is a little valley bathed in golden blushes.

A soldier, young, bareheaded, sleeps open-mouthed, his head
And shoulders bathing in the turquoise watercress;
Recumbent in the grass, pale in his verdant bed,
He sleeps; bright shafts of light like raindrops opalesce.

Feet in the gladioli, he sleeps. He wears a smile
Like that of a sick child; he slumbers all the while:
Nature, it's cold: cradle him warmly in his bed.

Even the fragrant air does not disturb his rest;
He sleeps beneath the sun, his hand upon his breast,
Peacefully. In his side two holes of vibrant red.

LE BATEAU IVRE

Comme je descendais des Fleuves impassibles,
Je ne me sentis plus guidé par les haleurs :
Des Peaux-Rouges criards les avaient pris pour cibles,
Les ayant cloués nus aux poteaux de couleurs.

J'étais insoucieux de tous les équipages,
Porteur de blés flamands ou de cotons anglais.
Quand avec mes haleurs ont fini ces tapages,
Les Fleuves m'ont laissé descendre où je voulais.

Dans les clapotements furieux des marées,
Moi, l'autre hiver, plus sourd que les cerveaux d'enfants,
Je courus ! Et les Péninsules démarrées
N'ont pas subi tohu-bohus plus triomphants.

La tempête a béni mes éveils maritimes.
Plus léger qu'un bouchon j'ai dansé sur les flots
Qu'on appelle rouleurs éternels de victimes,
Dix nuits, sans regretter l'oeil niais des falots !

Plus douce qu'aux enfants la chair des pommes sures,
L'eau verte pénétra ma coque de sapin
Et des taches de vins bleus et des vomissures
Me lava, dispersant gouvernail et grappin.

Et dès lors, je me suis baigné dans le Poème
De la Mer, infusé d'astres, et lactescent,
Dévorant les azurs verts ; où, flottaison blême
Et ravie, un noyé pensif parfois descend ;

Où, teignant tout à coup les bleuités, délires
Et rythmes lents sous les rutilements du jour,
Plus fortes que l'alcool, plus vastes que nos lyres,
Fermentent les rousseurs amères de l'amour !

THE DRUNKEN BOAT

As I serenely down impassive Rivers came,
I had a sense the haulers were no longer there:
Shrieking, whooping Redskins were practising their aim,
Having nailed them to posts after they'd stripped them bare.

I was indifferent toward the crewmen's fate,
Carriers of Flemish wheat or English cotton twill.
For once my haulers' noisy shouting did abate,
The Rivers were disposed to let me sail at will.

Into the furious surge of the unbridled tide,
Last winter I careered, deaf as an infant's brain!
And the Peninsulas, their moorings cast aside,
Had never known a hue and cry more unrestrained.

The tempest blessed my waking hours upon the sea.
More lightweight than a cork I gambolled to and fro,
Eternal victims' breakers they're supposed to be,
Nine nights I never missed the lantern's stupid glow!

Sweeter than to a child a bitter apple's flesh,
The emerald water poured into my pinewood frame
And dark blue stains of wine and blobs of nauseous retch
Washed over me, bestrewing grappling hook and helm.

And since that moment on, I have bathed in the Verse
Of the Sea, blent with stars, lactescent to the eye,
Devouring azures green; where, pallid, half submersed,
A drowned man caught in pensive rapture passes by;

Where, staining suddenly the azure, ardent fires
And languid rhythms neath the shimmer from above,
Stronger than alcohol, and vaster than our lyres,
Ferment the bitter russet anguishes of love!

LE BATEAU IVRE

Je sais les cieux crevant en éclairs, et les trombes
Et les ressacs et les courants : je sais le soir,
L'Aube exaltée ainsi qu'un peuple de colombes,
Et j'ai vu quelquefois ce que l'homme a cru voir !

J'ai vu le soleil bas, taché d'horreurs mystiques,
Illuminant de longs figements violets,
Pareils à des acteurs de drames très antiques
Les flots roulant au loin leurs frissons de volets !

J'ai rêvé la nuit verte aux neiges éblouies,
Baisers montant aux yeux des mers avec lenteurs,
La circulation des sèves inouïes,
Et l'éveil jaune et bleu des phosphores chanteurs !

J'ai suivi, des mois pleins, pareille aux vacheries
Hystériques, la houle à l'assaut des récifs,
Sans songer que les pieds lumineux des Maries
Pussent forcer le mufle aux Océans poussifs !

J'ai heurté, savez-vous, d'incroyables Florides
Mêlant aux fleurs des yeux de panthères à peaux
D'hommes ! Des arcs-en-ciel tendus comme des brides
Sous l'horizon des mers, à de glauques troupeaux !

J'ai vu fermenter les marais énormes, nasses
Où pourrit dans les joncs tout un Léviathan !
Des écroulements d'eaux au milieu des bonaces,
Et les lointains vers les gouffres cataractant !

Glaciers, soleils d'argent, flots nacreux, cieux de braises !
Échouages hideux au fond des golfes bruns
Où les serpents géants dévorés des punaises
Choient, des arbres tordus, avec de noirs parfums !

THE DRUNKEN BOAT

I know the skies, their lightning bolts, the tempest's might,
The currents and the surf: I know the evening too,
The Dawn exalted like a flock of doves in flight,
And I have sometimes seen what man just thought he knew!

I've seen the low sun with its eerie mystic rays,
Illuminating with long purple outstrung splats,
Resembling actors seen in very ancient plays,
The distant waves that roll their trembling shutter-slats!

I've dreamed of the green night bedazzled by the snows,
Kisses that rise unto the sea's eyes, slow and long,
The circulation of new saps that no man knows,
The waking yellow-blue of phosphorescent song!

I've followed, months on end, like herds of cows in heat,
The swell crashing against the reefs, untamed and free,
Without imagining the Marys' glowing feet
Could force a muzzle on the wheezing of the sea!

I've come upon amazing Floridas, strange lands
Where flowers blend with eyes of panthers clad in hides
Of human skin! Rainbows stretched tight as bridle bands
On glaucous herds where sea and ocean meet the skies!

I have seen where enormous everglades ferment,
Nets in the reeds where rots a whole Leviathan!
Waters cascading neath a tranquil firmament,
As distant cataracts into great chasms run!

Glaciers, silver suns, pearly waves, fiery skies!
Hideous shipwrecks in the depths of sombre rents
Where giant snakes whose flesh has been devoured by lice
Drop down, from twisted trees, with nauseating scents!

LE BATEAU IVRE

J'aurais voulu montrer aux enfants ces dorades
Du flot bleu, ces poissons d'or, ces poissons chantants.
– Des écumes de fleurs ont bercé mes dérades
Et d'ineffables vents m'ont ailé par instants.

Parfois, martyr lassé des pôles et des zones,
La mer dont le sanglot faisait mon roulis doux
Montait vers moi ses fleurs d'ombre aux ventouses jaunes
Et je restais, ainsi qu'une femme à genoux...

Presque île, ballottant sur mes bords les querelles
Et les fientes d'oiseaux clabaudeurs aux yeux blonds.
Et je voguais, lorsqu'à travers mes liens frêles
Des noyés descendaient dormir, à reculons !

Or moi, bateau perdu sous les cheveux des anses,
Jeté par l'ouragan dans l'éther sans oiseau,
Moi dont les Monitors et les voiliers des Hanses
N'auraient pas repêché la carcasse ivre d'eau ;

Libre, fumant, monté de brumes violettes,
Moi qui trouais le ciel rougeoyant comme un mur
Qui porte, confiture exquise aux bons poètes,
Des lichens de soleil et des morves d'azur ;

Qui courais, taché de lunules électriques,
Planche folle, escorté des hippocampes noirs,
Quand les juillets faisaient crouler à coups de triques
Les cieux ultramarins aux ardents entonnoirs ;

Moi qui tremblais, sentant geindre à cinquante lieues
Le rut des Béhémots et les Maelstroms épais,
Fileur éternel des immobilités bleues,
Je regrette l'Europe aux anciens parapets !

THE DRUNKEN BOAT

I would have liked to show to children those sea bream,
Fish of the azure sea, the golden fish that sings.
– Blown spumes bedecked with flowers rocked me as in a dream,
And ineffable winds would sometimes give me wings.

Sometimes, like martyrs, far from poles and zones to flee,
Rocking me gently with their sighs and sobs, the seas
Offered their golden cups of umbral flowers to me,
And I remained there, like a woman on her knees…

As if an island, tossing discord from my banks
And excrement from squawking birds with flaxen eyes;
And onwards did I drift, when through my fragile planks
Drowned men sank backwards down in somnolent demise!

So I, a boat beneath the hair of coves adrift,
Hurled into birdless skies by the storm-battered lave,
And neither Monitors nor Hanseatic craft
Would ever have seen fit my drunken hulk to save;

Smoking and free I went, in violet mists entwined,
I who transpierced the sky, red glowing like a wall
That wears, for worthy bards an elixir divine,
Lichens of sunshine and cerulean snots withal;

Who journeyed onward, by electric crescents stained,
A crazy plank, escorted by seahorses black as night,
When Julys brought destruction as their cudgels rained
Down blows on azure skies with funnels burning bright;

Who trembled when I sensed at fifty leagues the moans
Of Behemoths in rut, the Maelstroms and the squalls,
Eternal spinner of immobile azure tones,
How I miss Europe with its ancient city walls!

LE BATEAU IVRE

J'ai vu des archipels sidéraux ! et des îles
Dont les cieux délirants sont ouverts au vogueur :
– Est-ce en ces nuits sans fonds que tu dors et t'exiles,
Million d'oiseaux d'or, ô future Vigueur ?

Mais, vrai, j'ai trop pleuré ! Les Aubes sont navrantes.
Toute lune est atroce et tout soleil amer :
L'âcre amour m'a gonflé de torpeurs enivrantes.
Ô que ma quille éclate ! Ô que j'aille à la mer !

Si je désire une eau d'Europe, c'est la flache
Noire et froide où vers le crépuscule embaumé
Un enfant accroupi plein de tristesse, lâche
Un bateau frêle comme un papillon de mai.

Je ne puis plus, baigné de vos langueurs, ô lames,
Enlever leur sillage aux porteurs de cotons,
Ni traverser l'orgueil des drapeaux et des flammes,
Ni nager sous les yeux horribles des pontons.

THE DRUNKEN BOAT

I have seen astral archipelagos! and isles
Whose fevered skies are open to the drifter's course:
—Is it in these vast nights that you sleep in exile,
A million golden birds, O future Vital Force?

But I have wept too much! Each Dawn distresses me.
Each moon is hideous, each sun embitters me:
Sharp pangs of bitter love swell and bewilder me.
O let my keel fragment! O give me to the sea!

The one water in Europe I might wish to see
Would be the cold black mere where at the close of day
A pensive crouching child releases wistfully
A boat as fragile as a butterfly of May.

I can no more, O waves, bathed in your languid roll,
Take up the wash that transporters of cotton raise,
Nor undergo the pride of flags and banderoles,
Nor swim beneath the prison hulks' repulsive gaze.

ALPHABETICAL INDEX

A Parisian Dream	77
A Sentimental Colloquy	115
Album Leaf	103
Atonement	51
Autumn Song	111
Correspondences	65
Dawn is less clear...	45
Invitation to a Journey	71
It weeps in my heart...	117
My Familiar Dream	113
Oceano Nox	47
Ode to Cassandra	19
Reflection	67
Solitude	31
Sonnet for Helen	21
The Afternoon of a Faun	95
The Albatross	63
The Art of Poetry	107
The Balcony	69
The Drunken Boat	123
The Elf King	27
The Lake	35
The Sleeper in the Valley	121
The Voyage	81
To a Passer-by	75
Tomorrow, when the dawn...	43
Welcome and Farewell	25

www.ingramcontent.com/pod-product-compliance
Lightning Source LLC
Chambersburg PA
CBHW071227090426
42736CB00014B/3002